Assessment Guide

A Guide to the Fountas & Pinnell

Benchmark Assessment System 2

Irene C. Fountas

Gay Su Pinnell

Heinemann

Portsmouth, NH

Heinemann
361 Hanover St.
Portsmouth, NH 03801–3912
www.heinemann.com

Offices and agents throughout the world.

Fountas & Pinnell Benchmark Assessment System 2
Assessment Guide

Andrew Swaine: Cover (left), page1 (middle/bottom), 3-9, 11 (middle), 43 (middle/bottom),59 (middle), and 115 (bottom)
Mike Swendner: Cover (middle, right), page 1 (top), 11 (top/bottom), 29, 43 (top), 59 (top/bottom), 101 (top/middle/bottom), and 115 (top/middle)

ISBN-10: 0-325-01266-0
ISBN-13: 978-0-325-01266-7

Printed in China
2 3 4 5 6 7 8 NOR 15 14 13 12 11 10 09 08

Table of Contents

Table of Contents *(continued)*

About the *Fountas & Pinnell Benchmark Assessment System*

In this section, we provide background for benchmark assessment in general and its relationship to our work in particular. An overview of the Fountas & Pinnell Benchmark Assessment System components displays the file box and its contents and gives a brief description of all the parts of the System. Finally, we share ideas about how to prepare for an efficient assessment conference.

Introduction to the *Fountas & Pinnell Benchmark Assessment System*

Fountas & Pinnell Benchmark Assessment System 2 provides materials and procedures for observing and assessing the reading levels and behaviors of students in grades 3–8. It is directly linked to Fountas and Pinnell levels L–Z and small-group reading instruction using leveled books.

A *benchmark* is a standard against which to measure something. In *Fountas & Pinnell Benchmark Assessment System 2*, the standard is set by the benchmark books a student reads aloud and talks about during the assessment conference. These books have been written, edited, and extensively field-tested to ensure that they reflect the characteristics of texts and the demands of texts on the reader at each specific Fountas and Pinnell level.

Fountas and Pinnell levels, created and refined as a teaching and assessment tool over the past twenty years, represent twenty-six points on a gradient of reading difficulty (Figure 1). Each point on that gradient, from the easiest at level A to the most challenging at level Z, represents a small but significant increase in difficulty over the previous level. There are two benchmark books (a fiction and a nonfiction) for each of these levels from L–Z in *Fountas & Pinnell Benchmark Assessment System 2*. Following the Benchmark Assessment System's standardized assessment procedures, you use these leveled benchmark books to identify each student's reading levels. Benchmark results yield optimal levels for independent reading

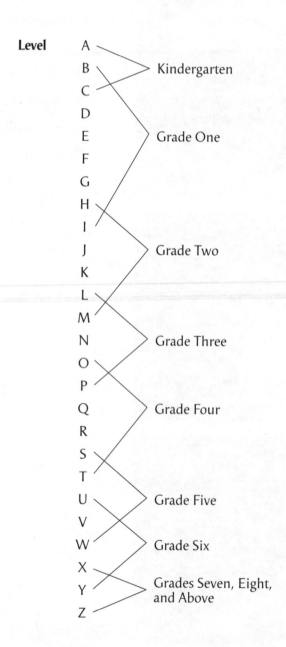

Figure 1. Gradient of Text

and instructional reading at one point in time. The results also provide information about the text level that will be too demanding to allow for effective learning by the student.

The Fountas & Pinnell Benchmark Assessment System is administered during a one-on-one, student-teacher assessment conference. For about thirty minutes, the student reads aloud and talks about a series of benchmark books while you observe and code the reader's behaviors on carefully constructed benchmark forms. Using established scoring conventions and procedures for analysis, you can not only establish optimal learning levels but also gather valuable information about each individual's reading processing, fluency, and comprehension—all of which give you insights about how to target your future teaching. Optional diagnostic assessments that focus on phonics/word analysis and vocabulary provide even more data to inform high-quality instruction.

Administered *once*, the Fountas & Pinnell Benchmark Assessment System conferences provide information to help you

▶ determine three reading levels for each student: Benchmark Independent, Benchmark Instructional, and Recommended Placement

▶ group students for reading instruction

▶ select texts that will be productive for a student's instruction

▶ plan efficient and effective instruction

▶ identify students who need intervention and extra help

▶ diagnose particular areas of reading difficulty

Administered *more than once* in a school year or across school years, the Fountas & Pinnell Benchmark Assessment System can do all of that *plus* document student progress across a school year and across grade levels. As readers progress through the levels, becoming increasingly competent readers, the A–Z gradient becomes a "ladder of progress."

There are two ways to preview the Fountas & Pinnell Benchmark Assessment System: by reading through this guide or by exploring the *Professional Development* DVD. You will also find helpful information at fountasandpinnell benchmarkassessment.com.

Components of the Fountas & Pinnell Benchmark Assessment System

All components of the system are conveniently packaged in a sturdy box that includes hanging file folders for the purpose of organizing the benchmark books and Recording Forms by level for easy access.

Benchmark Assessment System 2

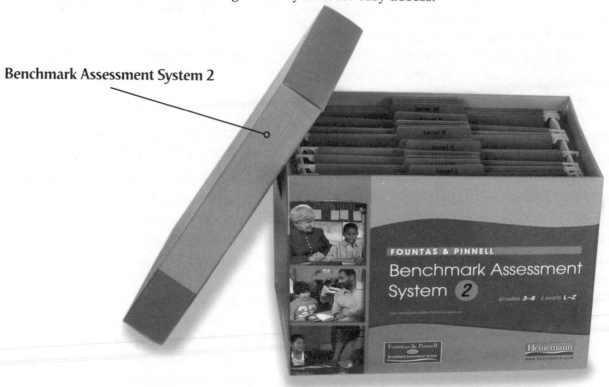

Benchmark Books

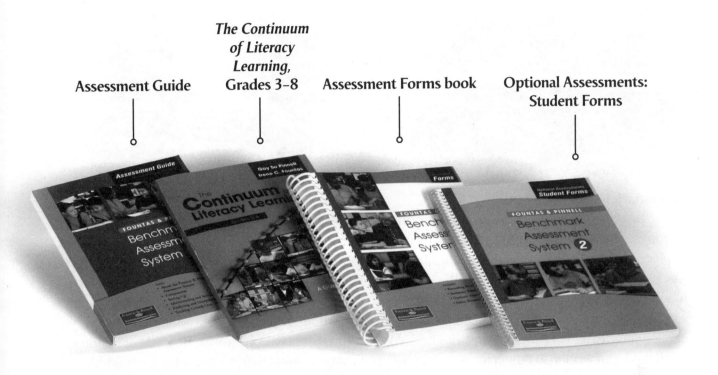

Assessment Guide

The Continuum of Literacy Learning, Grades 3–8

Assessment Forms book

Optional Assessments: Student Forms

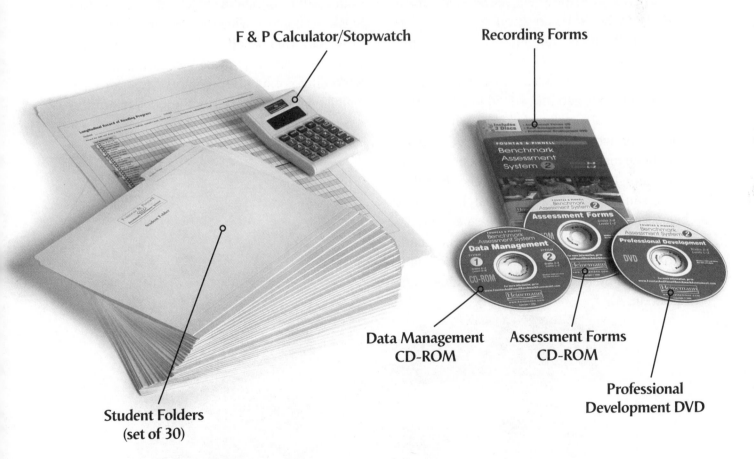

F & P Calculator/Stopwatch

Recording Forms

Student Folders (set of 30)

Data Management CD-ROM

Assessment Forms CD-ROM

Professional Development DVD

Benchmark Books

Thirty benchmark books, a fiction and a non-fiction text for each level from L–Z, are the centerpiece of the *Fountas & Pinnell Benchmark Assessment System 2* and provide the student reading contexts. They are organized from lowest (L) to highest (Z) level to reflect increasingly challenging texts. Each fiction and nonfiction book has been written to reflect the text characteristics specific to the level. (See *Leveled Books, K–8: Matching Texts to Readers for Effective Teaching* [Fountas and Pinnell, Heinemann, 2006] for a full description of these level characteristics.) In addition, each benchmark book has been field-tested and edited to ensure representation of the designated level, whether fiction or nonfiction. Fiction and nonfiction pairs have been matched so that if a student can read one genre, he should be able to read the other at the same level. (See the research report at fountasandpinnellbenchmarkassessment.com.)

The characteristics of all thirty benchmark books in the Fountas & Pinnell Benchmark Assessment System 2 are described in detail in Appendix A.

Assessment Forms Book and CD-ROM

All forms for the system are available in a book of blackline masters as well as in electronic form on a CD-ROM. Both the book and the CD-ROM contain resources that can be copied or printed in the quantities needed for assessment: Recording Forms and Assessment Summary forms, Class Record forms, Records of Reading Progress, At-a-Glance charts for easy administration, and optional assessments. On the CD-ROM, a simple navigation system allows you to select forms based on book level, title, and genre. An option is available to print out the Recording Forms in an enlarged font for easy legibility. Appendix B lists the contents of the *Assessment Forms* book and CD-ROM.

Professional Development DVD

The *Professional Development* DVD provides a foundation for understanding the Fountas & Pinnell Benchmark Assessment System materials and procedures. Its goal is to provide individualized training in coding, scoring, analyzing, and interpreting reading records and using the information to inform teaching. The DVD walks you through the parts of the program and the assessment administration procedures. It includes an overview of the program components; multiple models of teachers administering the benchmark assessment with students; and an in-depth discussion of scoring, analyzing, and interpreting an assessment. Practice sessions with sample assessment data provide you with opportunities to train yourself anywhere and any time on coding oral reading; scoring accuracy, fluency, and comprehension; and analyzing and interpreting results. The modular structure and interactive design of the DVD allow you to direct your own learning and focus on areas of greatest interest or need.

F & P Calculator/ Stopwatch

The specially designed F & P Calculator/Stopwatch performs highly specific functions related to the system. Input start and end times, running words, and number of errors and self-corrections, and the calculator will give you the reading time (time button), reading rate in words per minute (WPM button), accuracy percentage (Accur.% button), and the self-correction ratio (SC button).

Optional Assessments: Student Forms

This book provides a reusable student copy of the Where-to-Start Word Test and selected optional assessments (phonics and word analysis as well as vocabulary assessments). Turned to the appropriate assessment, it can be placed in front of the student for specific assessments. Each student page is laminated and arranged to make it easy for the reader to follow.

Student Folders

File folders designed to be used for each reader not only are a handy place to store recent assessment results and observations but also are printed with a Longitudinal Record of Reading Progress that can be passed from grade to grade, K–8.

Data Management CD-ROM

The *Data Management* CD-ROM enables you to manage benchmark assessment scores, analyze individual and group progress over time, and compare data from any component of the assessment within small groups or entire classes. The data are securely stored on a teacher's individual computer. The reports generated by the CD-ROM are customizable according to preferences set by the teacher and can be printed and shared with colleagues and administrators as needed. A district version of the data management software that allows longitudinal data tracking within and across schools will be available separately.

Preparing for Benchmark Assessment

Even before you begin getting ready to administer the assessment, you will want to think about when and where you'll want to conduct the one-on-one Fountas & Pinnell Benchmark Assessment System conference. If you are the student's literacy teacher, you are the ideal person to conduct the assessment, as you will gain firsthand a rich set of information to inform your teaching.

Get Started Quickly and Make a Schedule

Plan to begin your assessment conferences right at the start of the school year and spend about two weeks of your daily reading block time completing them. The assessment conference will give you a chance to spend time with each student. Get to know your students and begin to develop a relationship while you gather critical information. You can think of the assessment conference as time well spent on reading, thinking, and talking with students. You may also decide to have them do the writing portion of the assessment, giving them another opportunity to engage in a worthwhile literacy activity that provides evidence of text understanding.

Use Reading Block Time

We suggest that you conduct your assessment during your reading block times while the students are reading independently or engaged in other assigned independent literacy work. Plan to complete about two or three assessments per day. Some assessment conferences will be short, while others will be longer. This schedule will enable you to complete your series of assessment conferences in about two weeks.

Frequency of Assessment

It is important to determine each student's reading level at the start of the year. You may also want to reassess at year end or mid-year. If you are a middle school teacher, you may want to assess all your students or *only* the students reading below grade level, depending on the amount of time you have available. Then you would reassess only the students whose progress needs to be closely monitored.

Enlist School Support

You may have a teaching assistant, a student teacher, or a rotating substitute teacher in the school who can read aloud to the students, engage them in shared reading, or monitor independent work. This support will free you up to conduct two or three assessment conferences each day.

If your school is able to provide one or two days of substitute coverage, you will be able to assess most of your students. The substitute can provide instruction while you work efficiently to take each of your students for an assessment conference.

Another option is to pair up with a grade-level colleague so that one of you can teach students from both classes while the other conducts assessments with his own students.

Select a Location

Find a place that is reasonably quiet to administer the assessment system. You will not want the student to be distracted and you also want to hear the student's responses clearly. Some specialist teachers have their own instructional space that is empty when they do not have students, so they can take the student to the room where it is very quiet. On the other hand, it may not be worth going a lengthy distance down the hall.

We have had good experience with giving the assessment in a quiet corner of the classroom while other students are engaged in independent work. You may want to take this option (or work just outside the room in the corridor) if you have staff support. If you work in the classroom, you can have dedicated space in which you have your kit and all materials organized.

Be sure that you are conducting the assessment far enough away from the other students you are going to assess that they cannot hear you talking about the stories.

Put Materials in Order

The assessment will go more smoothly if you begin with everything prepared and in order.

▶ *Benchmark books.* Make sure the fiction and nonfiction benchmark books for each level are in the appropriate level folder in the benchmark kit. You can have the entire kit available (if you have space) or take out the levels that you plan to use.

▶ *Recording Forms.* Also in the hanging file folder, you will want to place multiple copies of all of the Recording Forms for both the fiction and the nonfiction benchmark books. These forms have the typed texts for each book and the space to record all of your information. Printing out multiple copies from the *Assessment Forms* CD-ROM or copying them from the book and keeping them in good supply in the hanging folders will save time going to the printer or copy machine for each assessment.

▶ *Assessment Summary.* You will want to have a supply of these generic forms, also found in the *Assessment Forms* book and CD-ROM, in a folder in the front of your kit. You'll need at least one copy to summarize the set of text readings for each student you assess.

▶ *F & P Calculator/Stopwatch.* While you can do the assessment without the F & P Calculator/Stopwatch (using the formulas included on the Recording Form), it will be quick and easy to have your F & P Calculator/Stopwatch with you.

▶ *At-a-Glance charts.* Two charts in the *Assessment Forms* book and CD-ROM will be helpful in reminding you of key steps in the assessment process. Make a copy of each to clip on your clipboard or laminate for your assessment corner. The Assessment at-a-Glance chart provides a concise description of the administration procedures. It will be helpful in reminding you of the steps, especially the first year you use the system. The Coding and Scoring at-a-Glance Chart provides a quick review of coding and scoring procedures for oral reading. Over time, you will be so familiar with this information that you will not need to use the cards. (The Assessment at-a-Glance Chart is also inside the front cover of this book and the Coding and Scoring at-a-Glance Chart is inside the back cover.)

▶ *Writing implements.* Have a good supply of writing implements—sharpened pencils or markers—so you will not have to spend time looking for them. We suggest that you use inexpensive mechanical pencils so you can erase if needed. If you choose to have students complete the optional drawing or writing section of the assessment, it will be more efficient to give the students a pencil or a thin marker rather than having them look for their own. A thin marker is ideal so students simply cross out when needed instead of spending time erasing.

Administering and Scoring the *Fountas & Pinnell Benchmark Assessment System*

In this section, you will find directions for administering the Fountas & Pinnell Benchmark Assessment System. You can print a spare version of these directions (Assessment-at-a-Glance) from the inside front cover or the *Assessment Forms* book or CD-ROM and place it in front of you as you conduct the assessment. You might want to copy it on card stock and laminate it or tape it in the area in which you conduct your assessment conferences. The *Professional Development* DVD offers additional guidance on how to administer, score, and analyze Benchmark Assessments.

We begin with a walk-through of the Recording Form, which is the System's primary tool for collecting and recording data about the child's oral reading and comprehension. Each book in the Fountas & Pinnell Benchmark Assessment System has a corresponding three-part Recording Form that guides the assessment procedures at all levels. It is used to observe and code the reading behavior through Oral Reading (Part One), a Comprehension Conversation (Part Two), and an optional Writing About Reading prompt for responding to the text (Part Three). The first four pages of this section present a brief summary of the form. A detailed explanation follows.

Recording Form Walk-Through

Part One: Oral Reading

The oral reading section of the assessment includes:

1 Space for the student's name, grade, the date of the assessment, the teacher's name, and the school's name. You'll have a Recording Form for each book a student reads.

2 A standardized text introduction to read aloud to the student after showing the student the benchmark book cover and reading aloud the title

3 A place to record the start and end time. You will use the reading time and the running words (RW) later to calculate reading rate or use the F & P Calculator/Stopwatch.

4 The typed text of the benchmark book appears word for word, page for page. On this text, you code the oral reading, recording errors (repetitions, substitutions, omissions, insertions) and self-corrections.

5 Columns to tally the reader's errors (E) and self-corrections (SC) with additional columns for analysis of these errors and self-corrections. Each of these attempts is analyzed for the source of information the reader likely used to make it: M = meaning, S = structure, and V = visual information.

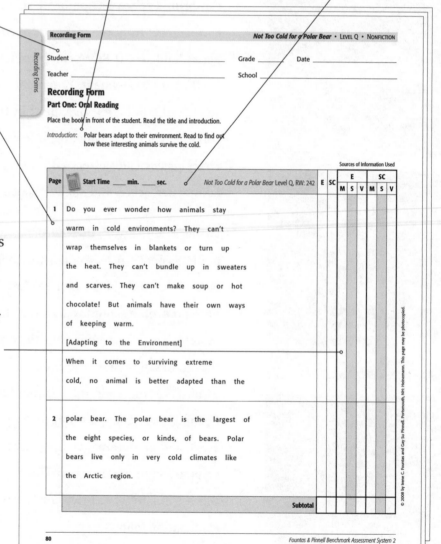

reading rate start at level J (p.13) instructional is where teaching begins

A scoring section summarizes the oral reading: accuracy, self-corrections, fluency, and reading rate.

6 A chart to help you quickly figure the accuracy rate (the percentage of the total words that the student has read correctly) by tallying the number of errors on the coded text and circling the errors and matching percentage on the scale

7 A space to record the num~~ber of~~ corrections (when the rea~~der makes~~ an error and then, without help from the teacher, corrects it)

8 A four-point (0–3) fluency scale and scoring key for evaluating fluency (the way the reading sounds), including phrasing, intonation, pausing, stress, rate, and integration

9 A place to record the reading rate, the number of words per minute (WPM) the student reads. The form provides the formula for calculating the reading rate, or you can use the F & P Calculator/Stopwatch.

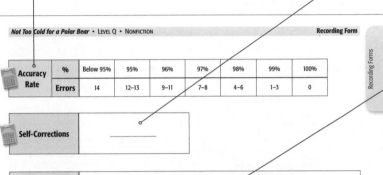

Not Too Cold for a Polar Bear • LEVEL Q • NONFICTION — Recording Form

Accuracy Rate	**%**	Below 95%	95%	96%	97%	98%	99%	100%
	Errors	14	12–13	9–11	7–8	4–6	1–3	0

Self-Corrections _____

Fluency Score   0 1 2 3

Fluency Scoring Key

0 Reads primarily word-by-word with occasional, but infrequent or inappropriate phrasing; no smooth or expressive interpretation, irregular pausing, and no attention to author's meaning or punctuation; no stress or inappropriate stress, and slow rate.

1 Reads primarily in two-word phrases with some three- and four- word groups and some word-by-word reading; almost no smooth or expressive interpretation and pausing guided by author's meaning and punctuation; almost no stress or inappropriate stress, with slow rate most of the time.

2 Reads primarily in three- or four-word phrase groups; some smooth expressive interpretation and pausing guided by author's meaning and punctuation; mostly appropriate stress and rate with some slow-downs.

3 Reads primarily in larger, meaningful phrases or word groups; mostly smooth, expressive interpretation and pausing, guided by author's meaning and punctuation; appropriate stress and rate with only a few slow-downs.

Reading Rate *(Optional)*

End Time ____ min. ____ sec.
Start Time ____ min. ____ sec.
Total Time ____ min. ____ sec.
Total Seconds ____

(198 × 60) ÷ Total Seconds = ____ Words Per Minute (WPM)

© 2008 by Irene C. Fountas and Gay Su Pinnell, Portsmouth, NH: Heinemann. This page may be photocopied.

Fountas & Pinnell Benchmark Assessment System 2 — 83

Recording Form Walk-Through, *continued*

Part Two: Comprehension Conversation

Immediately after the oral reading, and before the scoring is complete, you will engage the reader in a comprehension conversation about the benchmark book.

10 An open-ended invitation to talk to begin the comprehension conversation

11 A chart of key understandings, important ideas or thinking that the reader should have gained from *within* the text (getting the literal meaning by processing words and stated ideas), *beyond* the text (getting the implied meaning and synthesizing information), and *about* the text (engaging in critical analysis and responding to the writer's craft). The chart includes space to write in additional understandings the student demonstrates.

12 The chart also includes a column containing prompts to help you elicit the key understandings (important ideas) the reader may not have mentioned.

13 A comprehension scoring key that will guide you in scoring each category of key understandings on a four-point (0–3) scale in the score column

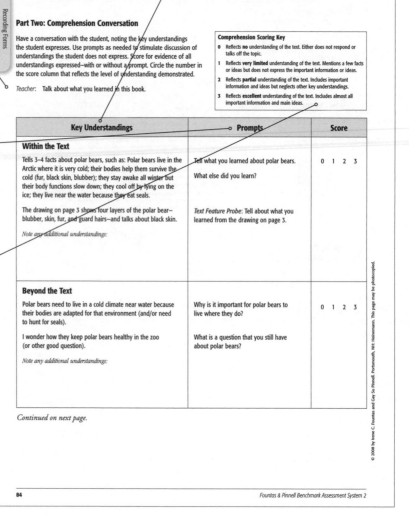

Recording Form   *Not Too Cold for a Polar Bear* • LEVEL Q • NONFICTION

Part Two: Comprehension Conversation

Have a conversation with the student, noting the key understandings the student expresses. Use prompts as needed to stimulate discussion of understandings the student does not express. Score for evidence of all understandings expressed—with or without a prompt. Circle the number in the score column that reflects the level of understanding demonstrated.

Teacher: Talk about what you learned in this book.

Comprehension Scoring Key

0 Reflects **no** understanding of the text. Either does not respond or talks off the topic.

1 Reflects **very limited** understanding of the text. Mentions a few facts or ideas but does not express the important information or ideas.

2 Reflects **partial** understanding of the text. Includes important information and ideas but neglects other key understandings.

3 Reflects **excellent** understanding of the text. Includes almost all important information and main ideas.

Key Understandings	Prompts	Score
Within the Text		
Tells 3–4 facts about polar bears, such as: Polar bears live in the Arctic where it is very cold; their bodies help them survive the cold (fur, black skin, blubber); they stay awake all winter but their body functions slow down; they cool off by lying on the ice; they live near the water because they eat seals. The drawing on page 3 shows four layers of the polar bear—blubber, skin, fur, and guard hairs—and talks about black skin. *Note any additional understandings:*	Tell what you learned about polar bears. What else did you learn? *Text Feature Probe:* Tell about what you learned from the drawing on page 3.	0 1 2 3
Beyond the Text		
Polar bears need to live in a cold climate near water because their bodies are adapted for that environment (and/or need to hunt for seals). I wonder how they keep polar bears healthy in the zoo (or other good question). *Note any additional understandings:*	Why is it important for polar bears to live where they do? What is a question that you still have about polar bears?	0 1 2 3

Continued on next page.

84   *Fountas & Pinnell Benchmark Assessment System 2*

© 2008 by Irene C. Fountas and Gay Su Pinnell. Portsmouth, NH: Heinemann. This page may be photocopied.

Part Three: Writing About Reading

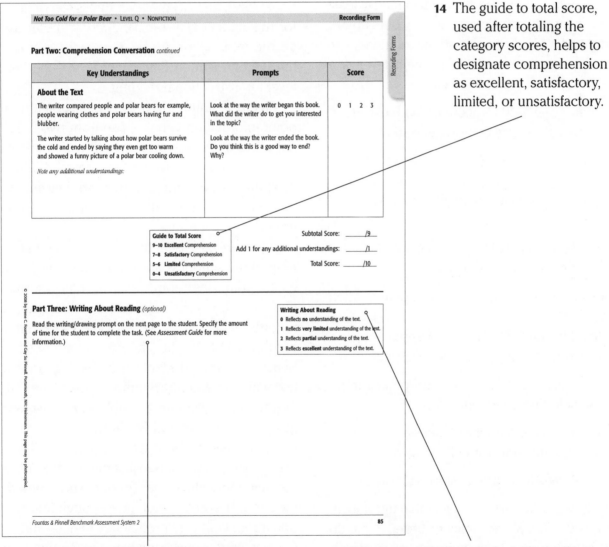

14 The guide to total score, used after totaling the category scores, helps to designate comprehension as excellent, satisfactory, limited, or unsatisfactory.

Not Too Cold for a Polar Bear • LEVEL Q • NONFICTION   **Recording Form**

Part Two: Comprehension Conversation *continued*

Key Understandings	Prompts	Score
About the Text		
The writer compared people and polar bears for example, people wearing clothes and polar bears having fur and blubber.	Look at the way the writer began this book. What did the writer do to get you interested in the topic?	0 1 2 3
The writer started by talking about how polar bears survive the cold and ended by saying they even get too warm and showed a funny picture of a polar bear cooling down.	Look at the way the writer ended the book. Do you think this is a good way to end? Why?	
Note any additional understandings:		

Guide to Total Score
9–10 Excellent Comprehension
7–8 Satisfactory Comprehension
5–6 Limited Comprehension
0–4 Unsatisfactory Comprehension

Subtotal Score: _____ /9

Add 1 for any additional understandings: _____ /1

Total Score: _____ /10

Part Three: Writing About Reading *(optional)*

Read the writing/drawing prompt on the next page to the student. Specify the amount of time for the student to complete the task. (See *Assessment Guide* for more information.)

Writing About Reading
0 Reflects **no** understanding of the text.
1 Reflects **very limited** understanding of the text.
2 Reflects **partial** understanding of the text.
3 Reflects **excellent** understanding of the text.

© 2008 by Irene C. Fountas and Gay Su Pinnell, Portsmouth, NH: Heinemann. This page may be photocopied.

Fountas & Pinnell Benchmark Assessment System 2   85

15 A prompt for the (optional) writing/drawing assessment designed to provide additional evidence of text comprehension

16 A four-point (0–3) scale for holistically scoring the writing about reading. A detailed rubric is provided on page 41 in this guide.

Finding a Place to Start

One way to save time and still get excellent assessment data from benchmark testing is to find a good level at which to start. If you do not have sufficient information from the student's previous teacher or school records to judge the starting point for the assessment, you may want to use the Where-to-Start Word Test in the *Assessment Forms* book or CD-ROM. It is a series of lists of increasingly difficult words, organized by grade level and designed to help you approximate the starting point.

You will always have the student read at least three texts as you determine the Benchmark Independent and Benchmark Instructional levels. The Recommended Placement level is a decision based on all the data.

▶ *Easy*—98–100% accuracy with excellent or satisfactory comprehension

▶ *Instructional*—95–97% accuracy with excellent or satisfactory comprehension *or* 98–100% accuracy with limited comprehension

▶ *Hard*—below 95% accuracy with any comprehension score

These levels are necessarily relational to each other.

Ideally, you will start the assessment on a level that is easy for the reader. This text:

▶ is likely to support effective processing, including comprehension

▶ allows the reader to process smoothly and with phrasing

▶ allows the reader to start with success

Ideally, you will start with a text that the student can read with 98% accuracy or better. If you do not have an easy level, move down the levels until you do. Then continue the assessment with increasingly more difficult books (higher levels).

You want to find the level at which the student reads with 95–97% accuracy and excellent or satisfactory comprehension (Benchmark Instructional level). Have the student continue to read until he reads with less than 95% accuracy or until he makes the number of errors (E) noted on the front of the book he is reading. If the student's comprehension drops below the criterion for limited comprehension, you can also stop moving up the levels.

When that happens, you will usually have three levels: (1) the highest level read independently, (2) the highest level read at an instructional level, and (3) the level that is too difficult for the student (hard text). *Then*, you can use all the information to make a decision about the Recommended Placement level—the best level for instructional reading.

Figure 2 summarizes the kinds of starting-point information you can use from two different kinds of literacy programs. If your students have been learning to read in a leveled books program, use column 1. If they are learning to read in a standard textbook program, use column 2.

If you are assessing the student at the beginning of the school year or when a student first enters your classroom, first consider information from last year's teacher and the student records. In Figure 2 we provide some thinking that will help you choose a place to start. Remember that students are reading *unseen* text with only a minimal introduction to the text. The reading level they are able to achieve will give you a very good idea of the kind of texts they can read without teacher support. If you are working with an English language learner at the beginning of the year (or one who is new to the school), you may not have enough information about language proficiency to determine a place to start. Conversing with the student over several days and informally trying out a few leveled texts will provide more information. You will want to follow your district policy regard-

Sources of Information for Determining Assessment Starting Point (Independent Level)	
Leveled Books Program	**Core or Basal Program**
Use records or book charts from previous school year.	Use records from previous school year (see Figure 3 for conversion to Fountas and Pinnell level).
Identify books the student is reading independently (see *Fountas and Pinnell Leveled Book List, K–8* [Heinemann, 2006] or fountasandpinnellleveledbooks.com) for level, and start one level lower.	Identify books the student is reading independently (see *Fountas and Pinnell Leveled Book List* or fountasandpinnellleveledbooks.com) for level, and start one level lower.
Identify instructional-level books the student is reading in a reading group and move down one level.	Identify instructional-level book the student is reading (see Figure 4 for conversion to Fountas and Pinnell levels).
Use Where-to-Start Word Test (*Assessment Forms* book and CD-ROM; *Optional Assessments: Student Forms* book).	Use Where-to-Start Word Test (*Assessment Forms* book and CD-ROM; *Optional Assessments: Student Forms* book).
For English language learners, consider any information you have on language proficiency assessments. Also, all of the above information will be helpful in determining where to start.	For English language learners, consider any information you have on language proficiency assessments. Also, all of the above information will be helpful in determining where to start.

Figure 2. Sources of information for determining assessment starting point

ing language proficiency requirements and the administration of standardized tests prior to administering the Benchmark Assessment System. We believe you will find the small, precise differences in the benchmark book levels very useful in gathering information about the reading skills of English language learners.

If you are assessing at the middle or end of the school year, one of the best sources of information about where to start comes from the student's current reading performance in the classroom. If you are the classroom or literacy teacher and you have worked with the student recently, then you probably have a good idea of his instructional level. If you are not the classroom or literacy teacher, you can ask for advice about the level the student is reading. Figure 3 shows how you might determine a starting level at the beginning, middle, and end of the school year when the student's general reading performance is known.

Approximate Start Level Based on Expected Grade-Level Performance

Grade	Reading Performance (how the student is reading relative to expected grade-level performance)	Time of Year			Approximate Benchmark Assessment Starting Level
		Beg.	Mid.	End	
Grade 3	Below level	X			L*
	Below level		X		L*
	Below level			X	L*
	On level	X			M–N
	On level		X		M–N
	On level			X	N–O
	Above level	X			O–P
	Above level		X		P–Q
	Above level			X	Q–R
Grade 4	Below level	X			M–N
	Below level		X		N–O
	Below level			X	O–P
	On level	X			O–P
	On level		X		P–Q
	On level			X	Q–R
	Above level	X			R–S
	Above level		X		S–T
	Above level			X	U–V
Grade 5	Below level	X			Q–R
	Below level		X		R–S
	Below level			X	S–T
	On level	X			R–S
	On level		X		S–T
	On level			X	T–U
	Above level	X			U–V
	Above level		X		V–W
	Above level			X	W–X

Figure 3. Approximate start level based on expected grade-level performance

Continued on next page

Approximate Start Level Based on Expected Grade-Level Performance					
Grade	**Reading Performance** *(how the student is reading relative to expected grade-level performance)*	**Time of Year**			**Approximate Assessment Starting Level**
		Beg.	**Mid.**	**End**	
Grade 6	Below level	X			R–S
	Below level		X		S–T
	Below level			X	T–U
	On level	X			U–V
	On level		X		V–W
	On level			X	W–X
	Above level	X			W–X
	Above level		X		X–Y
	Above level			X	X–Y
Grade 7/8	Below level	X			S–T
	Below level		X		T–U
	Below level			X	U–V
	On level	X			W–X
	On level		X		X
	On level			X	Y
	Above level	X			X
	Above level		X		Y
	Above level			X	Z

Figure 3. Approximate start level based on expected grade-level performance, *continued*

*If L is too difficult for the reader, go to Benchmark System 1 and select a starting point based on the classroom teacher's estimate of student performance.

**If a student can read level Z with 98% or greater accuracy, satisfactory or excellent comprehension, and satisfactory fluency (Independent level), you will want to give the student opportunities to read a variety of books at X, Y, or Z that offer interesting topics and a broad array of genres.

Basal Anthology or Core Text User's Guide for Assessment	
Last Basal/Core Level the Student Completed	**Approximate Fountas & Pinnell Level to Start Testing**
Kindergarten	A
Grade 1 pre-primer (1)	B
Grade 1 pre-primer (2)	C
Grade 1 pre-primer (3)	D
Grade 1 primer	E
Grade 1 late	F
Grade 2 early	G
Grade 2 late	K
Grade 3 early	L
Grade 3 late	N
Grade 4 early	O
Grade 4 late	Q
Grade 5 early	R
Grade 5 late	T
Grade 6 early	U
Grade 6 late	V
Grade 7–8	W

Figure 4. Basal or core text user's guide for assessment

If you are using a basal or core program, you can also use the chart in Figure 4 to help you decide where to start. It will be helpful to think about the level of the basal core text or anthology your students have completed successfully and its correspondence to the Fountas and Pinnell levels (see Figure 4).

You may also opt to use the Where-to-Start Word Test, which is described in Appendix B and found in the *Assessment Forms* book and CD-ROM. This word test gives you a quick way to identify a starting point.

After determining the starting level—the highest level at which you expect the student will read with relative ease—locate the appropriate books in the benchmark kit and make sure you have copies of the Recording Forms for books at the selected level and for the levels before and after it from the *Benchmark Assessment Forms* book or CD-ROM. The fiction and nonfiction texts for each level are listed in Figure 5.

For each level, you have a fiction and a nonfiction text. The level of the book appears in two places on every book: (1) on the front cover in the lower left corner and (2) on the back cover in the lower left corner. These labbels will help you easily locate the appropriate book for the levels you have chosen. The genre of the book (fiction or nonfiction) is printed under the level on the lower left corner of the back cover. Fiction and nonfiction pairs have been matched so that if a student can read one genre, he is likely to be able to read the other. We recommend that you vary the fiction and nonfiction texts as you move up the gradient during an assessment conference, so if you begin with the fiction title, move on to a nonfiction title at the next level tested. This will give you a picture of how the student is performing in both genres.

	Benchmark 2 Books	
Level	**Fiction**	**Nonfiction**
L	*Ernie Learns*	*Hang On, Baby Monkey*
M	*Saving Up*	*City Hawks*
N	*Vanessa's Butterfly*	*Dogs at Work*
O	*The New Girl*	*Snake Myths*
P	*Plenty of Pets*	*Animal Instincts*
Q	*A Secret Home*	*Not Too Cold for a Polar Bear*
R	*The Election*	*Fishing Smarts*
S	*Could Be Worse*	*Amazing Animal Adaptations*
T	*"Get a Horse!"*	*Why Do Wolves Howl?*
U	*Canyon Mystery*	*Earthquakes*
V	*A Call for Change*	*Tsunamis: Mighty Ocean Waves*
W	*How I Spent My Summer Vacation*	*Obituary: Coretta Scott King 1927–2006*
X	*A Weighty Decision*	*The Internet: Getting Connected*
Y	*Saying Goodbye*	*The International Space Station*
Z	*Surviving the Blitz*	*The Train at the Top of the World*

Figure 5. Benchmark 2 books

Using the Assessment at-a-Glance Chart

For a quick reference, we suggest you copy the Assessment at-a-Glance Chart on the inside cover of this book, or print it from the *Assessment Forms* book or CD-ROM. The following sections take you step-by-step through the assesment conference.

Introducing the Benchmark Book

Read the title of the book. Then **read the standardized introduction** to the reader. The standardized introduction to the text is printed on the colored wave at the bottom of the front cover and on the Recording Form. The introductions were created and field-tested to give the reader a start on the book and to ensure that each student would begin the assessment with the same introductory material. For the assessment to be standardized, you will want to take care not to embellish the introduction or enter into any additional conversation with the student about the text.

If you are using the F & P Calculator/ Stopwatch, **enter the number of running words** (RW), which is printed on the book cover (Figure 6) and the Recording Form. The number of running words is the exact number of words that the student reads orally. It does not include the title of the book, captions under pictures, or words in speech balloons. This number is used to calculate the percentage of accuracy with which the student has read and the reading rate, which is the words per minute. The back cover has the total running words (TRW).

Note the number of errors printed under the running words on the front cover. It indicates the point at which the reader's accuracy has gone below 95%. When the accuracy rate goes below 95%, the text is probably too hard. Keeping track of the number of errors as a student reads will allow you to switch to a lower level if the reader is having much difficulty. You will need to judge whether to have the student finish reading the book or whether you want to discontinue the reading because the text is much too difficult.

Coding Oral Reading

Begin oral reading and timing. Have the student begin to read the text orally. Start the time on the F & P Calculator/ Stopwatch. Alternatively, you can start your stopwatch or use a clock with a second hand and record the starting time on the Recording Form. Have the student read to the stopping point and then continue to read silently. The stopping point is marked in the text (a black square) to show the point at which the student stops reading orally (see Figure 7).

Introduction
Running words
Number of errors

Figure 6. Benchmark book cover

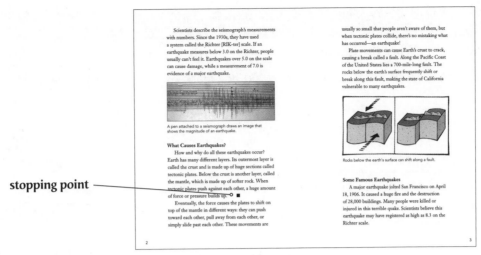

Figure 7. Stopping point for oral reading

Have the student read orally up to the stopping point while you code the behavior on the form. Then have the student continue to read silently. You can use this time to write comments and summarize the reading behaviors you observe.

Code the oral reading behavior on the Recording Form as the student reads. The page number and typed text on the Recording Form correspond exactly to the benchmark book, and there is space to record the student's errors and self-corrections. Record your observations using the conventions in Figure 9 on the next page. (The *Professional Development* DVD provides individualized training on the coding conventions.) Figure 8 shows how the coding might look partway through a student's oral reading of *Not Too Cold for a Polar Bear*.

Be sure to listen to how the reading sounds while you code errors, since you will simultaneously be evaluating accuracy (percentage of errors), judging fluency (the way the reading sounds), and using the timer to determine reading time. With especially fluent readers, you may get behind in your coding. If you get very far behind, you can ask the reader to stop and wait a moment at the end of a page. Or, if your coding is mixed up, you can ask the student to start over at a good point.

When the student has reached the stopping point, **stop timing** and record the time on the form.

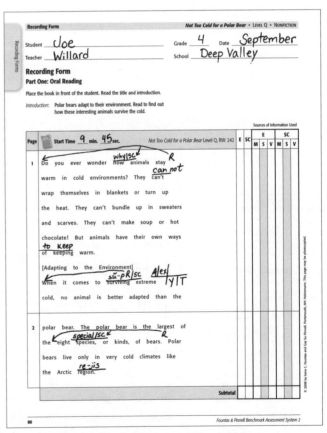

Figure 8. Coding oral reading of *Not Too Cold for a Polar Bear*

Coding			
Behavior	**What the Reader Does**	**Instruction**	**Code**
Accurate reading	Reads word correctly.	Do not mark word *or* place a check above the word.	no mark ✓ / environments
Substitution	Reads a word incorrectly.	Write the substitution above the word.	worry / wonder
Multiple substitutions	Makes several attempts at a word.	Write each of the substitutions in sequence above the word.	speckled/spices/specials / species
Self-correction	Corrects a previous error.	Write the error above the word, followed by *SC*.	adopted | SC / adapted
Insertion	Adds a word that is not in the text.	Write in the inserted word using a caret.	it's very / ʌ wet
Omission	Gives no response to a word.	Place a dash (–) above the word.	— / only
Repetition	Reads the same word again.	Write *R* after the word.	too R
Repeated repetitions	Reads the same word more than once.	Write *R* for the first repetition and then write a number for the additional repetitions.	too R₂
Rereading	Returns to the beginning of a sentence or phrase to read it again.	Write an *R* with an arrow back to the place where rereading began.	How do R
Appeal and "You try it"	Student verbally asks for help (A); teacher responds "You try it."	Write *A* above the word and *Y* after the word.	A / environments | Y
Told	Teacher tells student the word after attempt, appeal, and "You try it."	Write *T* after the word.	A / environments | Y | T
Spelling aloud	Student spells word by saying names of letters.	Write the letters in all capital letters with hyphens between them.	E-V-E-R / ever
Sounding out	Student makes the sounds associated with the letters in the word.	Write the letters in lowercase with hyphens between them.	o-n-l-y / only

Figure 9. Coding conventions for oral reading

Coding system developed by Marie Clay as part of the running record system in *An Observation Survey of Early Literacy Achievement, Revised Second Edition,* Heinemann, 2006.

Counting Errors to Get an Accuracy Score

Accuracy, the percentage of total words the student has read correctly, is only one indicator of a reader's ability to process a text, but it is an important one. Students may read a text with high accuracy but understand it only superficially. They may read a text with lower accuracy but remember enough details to get the gist. But in general, there is a relationship between accuracy and understanding.

Since this is a standardized assessment, you will want to use established guidelines to count errors and assess all of your students in the same way. In fact, it is important for all teachers in a school and district to use the same system. The error-counting conventions in Figure 10 on the next page will help you standardize the assessment for all students so that progress can be accurately documented. The chart shows the conventions and how to look at each behavior to count errors and self-corrections.

Special Cases

- If the student skips a full page of print, intervene and tell him to read the page. Do not count this as an error.

- If the student inserts many words, you could have more errors than the running words on a page. This is likely to happen only at the lower levels. In this case, score the page as having the same number of errors as words on the page.

- No matter how many attempts a student makes at a word, score only one error for each word.

- Occasionally, especially at the lower levels, a student will begin to "invent" text, that is, tell the story by making up his own language, disregarding the print. If this happens, write *inventing* at the top of the sheet and stop the assessment. In this case, the text is a hard text.

- When a reader is processing the text satisfactorily but gets mixed up and loses his place, just ask him to start over at a good starting point and begin your coding again. Do not count this as an error.

- If you are using this assessment with a student who is an English language learner, you will need to be sure that the student speaks English well enough to understand the directions and the introduction, enter into conversation with you, process the print, and understand the text. Estimate the level and move down if necessary. If the student seems confused, read the introduction again. You can also paraphrase directions as well as the comprehension conversation to support greater understanding.

Errors and Self-Corrections

Behavior	Coding	Error Counting
Accurate reading	nomark or <u>environments</u> ✓	No error
Substitution, not corrected	<u>worry</u> wonder	One error
Substitution, self-corrected	<u>worry|SC</u> wonder	No error; one SC
Multiple substitutions, not corrected	<u>adopt | adopted</u> adapted	One error per word in the text
Missing the same word several times in a text	<u>speckler</u> <u>spiced</u> species species	One error each time missed
Errors on names and proper nouns—repeated during the reading	<u>area</u> <u>ark</u> Arctic Arctic	One error the first time; no error after that even if different substitutions are made for the nouns
Contractions (reads as two words or reads two words as contraction)	<u>cannot</u> <u>they're</u> can't they are	One error
Multiple substitutions, self-corrected	<u>adopt | adopted | SC</u> adapted	No error; one SC
Insertion of a word	very it's ∧ <u>wet</u>	One error per word inserted
Omission of a word	<u>only</u>	One error per word
Skipping a line	<u>from the cold water</u>	One error per word
Repetition	R	No error
"You try it" followed by student reading correctly	✓ <u>environments | Y</u>	No error
"You try it" followed by a substitution	<u>endings</u> environments | Y	One error
"You try it" followed by Told	environments | Y | T	One error
Told (teacher supplied word)	environments | Y | T	One error
"Sounding out" followed by correct reading	<u>o-n-l-y | ✓</u> only	No error; no SC
"Sounding out" followed by incorrect or no further reading	<u>o-n-l-y | once</u> only	One error
Sounding the first letter and then saying the word correctly	<u>o-nly | ✓</u> only	No error; no SC
Sounding the first letter incorrectly and then saying the word correctly	<u>w— | SC</u> only	No error; one SC

Figure 10. Error and self-correction conventions

Coding system developed by Marie Clay as part of the running record system in *An Observation Survey of Early Literacy Achievement, Revised Second Edition*, Heinemann, 2006.

Total the errors and self-corrections in each line of text separately. A self-correction is *not* an error. Then count the errors by going down the column (see Figure 11).

Next, **figure out the accuracy score**. Enter the number of errors into the calculator and tap the accuracy button to get the percentage of words read accurately. Alternatively, on each Recording Form, you will find an accuracy graph (see Figure 12). This graph will help you instantly calculate the accuracy. Just count the errors and circle the accuracy that is relevant. Next, count the self-corrections and write the total number on the self-corrections line.

If the student is reading a level with less than 95% accuracy, you will want consider whether to continue with the comprehension conversation. If accuracy is below but close to 95% and there are repeated errors, the student may have understood enough that the comprehension conversation will provide important information. However, if the accuracy rate is well below the criterion and the student had much difficulty, you will want to end the assessment on this text. The level would be "hard."

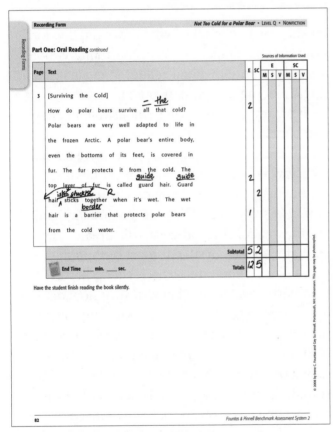

Figure 11. Counting errors and self-corrections

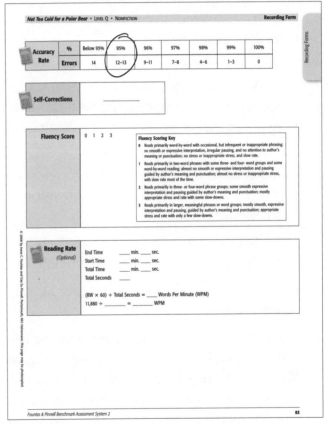

Figure 12. Accuracy score

Evaluating Fluency

Immediately after the student finishes reading orally, **rate fluency** by making a note at the bottom of the coded text of how the reading sounded and circling the rating on the fluency scoring key. The fluency score reflects how consistently students are interpreting the meaning of the text with their voices. When reading at the independent or instructional level, students should read along at a reasonable pace. At the instructional level, you can expect fluent, phrased reading, though at the independent level, reading will be more consistently fluent throughout the text. Use the following guidelines to rate readers' fluency. A high score indicates that the reader is

▶ phrasing, or grouping words, as evident through intonation, stress, and pauses as well as through emphasizing the beginnings and endings of phrases by rise and fall of pitch or by pausing

▶ adhering to the author's syntax or sentence structure, reflecting their comprehension of the language

▶ expressive; the student's reading reflects feeling, anticipation, and character development

▶ using punctuation to cue pausing or altering the voice

A simple four-point (0–3) fluency scoring key is included on the form and shown in Figure 13. Score fluency from 0–3 according to this key. (An optional, expanded Six Dimensions Fluency Rubric is included in the *Assessment Forms* book and CD-ROM.)

For reliable assessment across your school or district, view the examples of oral readings on the *Professional Development* DVD with a group of colleagues. Reach agreement on typical examples of ratings and then check with the ratings we have given. Once your group has built an internal sense of what each rating

Fluency Scoring Key

0 Reads primarily word-by-word with occasional but infrequent or inappropriate phrasing; no smooth or expressive interpretation, irregular pausing, and no attention to author's meaning or punctuation; no stress or inappropriate stress, and slow rate.

1 Reads primarily in two-word phrases with some three- and four-word groups and some word-by-word reading; almost no smooth, expressive interpretation or pausing guided by author's meaning and punctuation; almost no stress or inappropriate stress, with slow rate most of the time.

2 Reads primarily in three- or four-word phrase groups; some smooth, expressive interpretation and pausing guided by author's meaning and punctuation; mostly appropriate stress and rate with some slowdowns.

3 Reads primarily in larger, meaningful phrases or word groups; mostly smooth, expressive interpretation and pausing, guided by author's meaning and punctuation; appropriate stress and rate with only a few slowdowns.

Figure 13. Benchmark Assessment System fluency scoring key

means, you can quickly write down a rating for each record. Remember that the rating is not a label for an individual reader. It evaluates a single reading of a particular text.

Typically, a reader will demonstrate fluency and phrasing on texts that are easier (a score of 3). On more challenging texts, the same reader will slow down occasionally for problem solving but become more fluent on easier stretches of text (a score of 2). On texts that are too hard for the reader, the process will break down so that it sounds dysfluent most of the time (a score of 1). There are some readers, however, who have developed a habit of very slow reading. These readers may read with high accuracy but get low scores for fluency (a score of 0 or 1). On the other hand, some readers may gloss over errors or make careless errors, sounding fluent (a score of 3) but reading with low accuracy (below 95%). Each of these readers needs different instruction. Your diagnosis of a reader's fluency, viewed in the perspective of accuracy and comprehension scores, will provide information to inform teaching. Think about the reading as a whole and make a judgment as to the extent it was fluent and phrased. Remember that on an instructional-level text, the reader may slow down to problem solve and then speed up again.

Fluency and English Language Learners

It is important to note that when they read orally, many English language learners will not sound precisely the same as native speakers of the language. The cadence of the reading may vary slightly, or different words may be stressed. There may be pauses to search for the meaning of an English word or to translate meaning to the individual's first language. Phonetic variations that do not interfere greatly with comprehension or fluency can be ignored. Make a judgment based on your knowledge of the student and your conversation with him.

Also, it is good to remember that sometimes an individual may sound fluent when reading in a new language because she has learned to decode the words. You will want to check understanding very carefully. Just because a reader can decode the words and read with a fair amount of fluency does not guarantee understanding, and that is true of all learners.

Guiding the Comprehension Conversation

Often comprehension is assessed by asking the student a series of questions and checking the answers with a guide. Too often this can lead to students' thinking that they read to be able to answer the teacher's questions. For this assessment system, we have constructed a different process, one that will let you gather evidence of comprehension while engaging the student in a conversation about the text. As much as possible, the assessment activities should represent a reading conference. The student reads texts, converses with you about them, and then may do some writing about the text. As a general rule, you will want to complete the comprehension conversation on easy, instructional-level, and hard text. However, you may decide not to complete the comprehension conversation if the text is much too hard for the reader

(far below the standard for instructional reading) as you have strong evidence that the student did not likely understand it.

The Recording Form for each benchmark book provides a list of key understandings in the text, prompts that parallel those key understandings, and a score range (see Figures 14 and 15) for each type of thinking.

Understandings are categorized as:

▶ Evidence that the reader is thinking *within* the text. The reader is gaining the literal meaning of the text through solving the words, monitoring his own understanding and accuracy, searching for and using information, remembering information in summary form, adjusting for purpose and type of text, and sustaining fluent reading.

▶ Evidence that the reader is thinking *beyond* the text. The reader is making predictions; making connections with prior knowledge, personal experience, and other texts; inferring what is implied but not stated; and synthesizing new information by changing his own ideas.

▶ Evidence that the reader is thinking *about* the text. The reader is thinking about the literary elements of the text, recognizing elements of the writer's craft, and thinking critically about the text.

Once the student has completed the oral reading and you have determined that the text was not too difficult, **read the teacher's conversation starter** on the Recording Form to begin the conversation: "Talk about what happened in this story" or "Talk about what you learned in this book." The idea is to open a conversation that will allow you to see what the text has prompted the student to think. Be sure

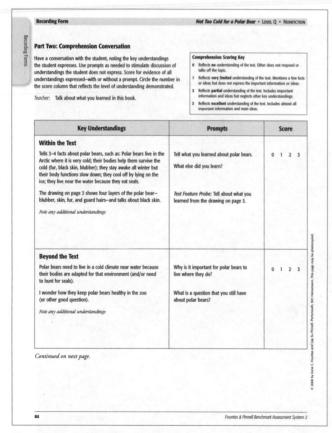

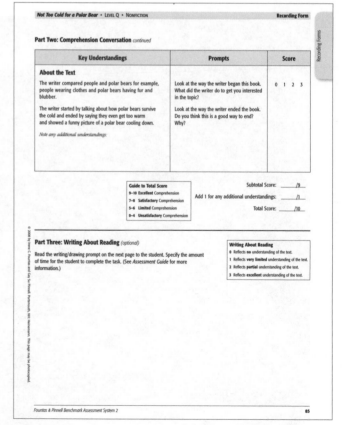

Figure 14. *Not Too Cold for a Polar Bear* comprehension conversation

Figure 15. *Not Too Cold for a Polar Bear* comprehension conversation

the student understands that *he* is expected to talk; some readers may think they are simply to listen or answer questions. Use conversational language to facilitate expansion of the student's talk. For example:

▶ "Say more about that."

▶ "What else?"

▶ "Can you talk more about that?"

▶ "What do you think about that?"

▶ "Say more about your thinking."

▶ "Say more."

▶ "Tell more about that."

▶ "Why do you think that?"

▶ "And then . . . ?"

▶ "And then what happened?"

▶ "And . . ."

Often, just pausing a few seconds more to listen will also prompt the student to say more. Too often we don't give the students enough wait time to formulate a response.

Note: It is acceptable for readers to search back in the written texts for answers to prompts and questions if they initiate the action. Leave the book in front of the reader and allow him to use the text, but don't make the suggestion. Also, if a student reads the text orally to respond, ask him not to read from the book but to tell his answer in his own words.

As you listen and interact, you will find evidence of many of the key understandings. **Place a checkmark next to the key understandings** in the left column as the evidence occurs in conversation (see Figure 16). Remember that you are not looking for word-for-word repetition of the understanding but rather for an indication that the reader understands the key idea. As you work with the Benchmark Assessment System, you will find it easy to detect specific evidence of understandings. If during your

comprehension conversation a student discusses insights and information that are not reflected in the key understandings on the form, **jot down additional understandings** the student volunteers. You can evaluate them later as part of the scoring.

If the reader does not mention some of the key understandings on his own, **use the prompts** in the middle column to probe further. You can ask questions or ask the student to talk more about a topic to elicit evidence of understanding and check it off on the form. You can paraphrase the questions if needed. Do not judge the student's response lower because you have to prompt for thinking. Prompted responses are just as correct as spontaneous ones. Many students are not accustomed to spontaneously talking about their understandings of texts. They have learned to wait for the questions. If the student is able to articulate thinking, consider its value whether prompted

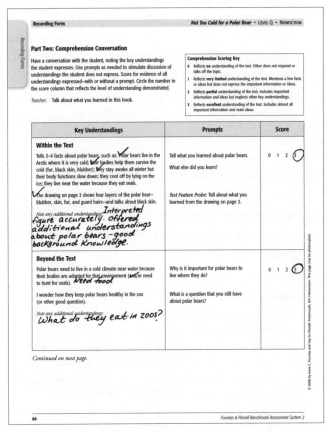

Figure 16. Recording evidence during the comprehension conversation

or not. At the same time, avoid "leading" the student to an answer. Just use the prompt in a conversational way and move on if the student cannot respond.

As you engage in this process with English language learners, make an extra effort to draw them into conversation, always realizing that the reader may understand more than she is able to explain in English. If you understand some of the student's own language, it is a great idea to converse for a few minutes using that language. But that is not always possible given the multitude of languages in our schools. Sketching may be helpful to the English language learner in expressing understandings. Also, time to write about the text may be easier for some students than talking immediately after reading. You can consider the student's sketching and writing in making a final decision about comprehension.

Scoring the Comprehension Conversation

After the comprehension conversation, **use the comprehension scoring key** (Figure 17) to judge the degree to which the student has demonstrated understanding of the text's key ideas and circle the appropriate number for each category: within, beyond, and about. This scale is not designed to "count" answers to questions in each category. Instead, make a judgment using the evidence in each of the three broad areas as to whether the reader showed unsatisfactory, limited, satisfactory, or excellent understanding of the text.

Comprehension Scoring Key

0 Reflects unsatisfactory understanding of the text. Either does not respond or talks off the topic.

1 Reflects limited understanding of the text. Mentions a few facts or ideas but does not express the important information or ideas.

2 Reflects satisfactory understanding of the text. Includes important information and ideas but neglects other key understandings.

3 Reflects excellent understanding of the text. Includes almost all important information and main ideas.

Figure 17. Comprehension scoring key

Make this judgment based on the scores and your overall impression after conversing with the reader, using the descriptions in the comprehension scoring key as a guide.

As you consider scoring, be sure that you have clear evidence of understanding. Remember that this score will be an important indicator of the kind of teaching that you need to do later.

Score additional understandings. Comprehension is such an individual factor that it is difficult to list the *exact* understandings that every reader should have. After analyzing the text, we can come up with some basic understandings that we think every reader should have; but each of us may actually take something different from a text based on our own life experiences. If your reader came up with one or more unique and valuable additional understandings, add a point to the comprehension score.

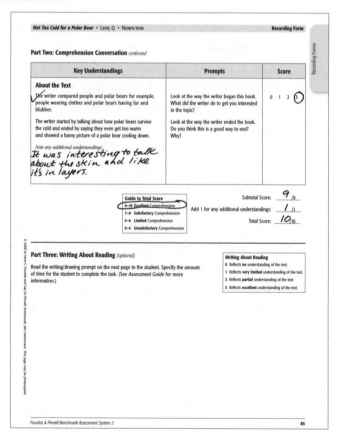

Figure 18. A scored comprehension conversation

Finally, add up the subscores and **use the guide to total score** to determine if the student's overall understanding was excellent, satisfactory, limited, or unsatisfactory (see Figure 18).

Making the Most of the Comprehension Conversation

After practicing a few of these comprehension conversations, you will find that the process is both easy and enjoyable. They are similar to the kinds of conversations you have every day with students in reading groups or reading conferences. Over time, your students will learn how to spontaneously offer their thinking about a text—and that is a valuable strategy to have.

What is a conversation like? If we observed you and a friend, we would likely see something like this:

1 You say something.

2 Your friend comments on what you said.

3 You add more.

4 Your friend asks a question.

5 You answer and make another comment.

6 Your friend says more.

We contrast this scene with a series of continuous questions that are asked one after another. The point is that real conversation does involve some questions but not a steady barrage. The conversation is a flow of talk, back and forth.

Try to engage the student in showing her thinking about the text. We have suggested open-ended prompts like "Say more about that" to invite the student to talk more about what she understood. You may also want to use a specific question. Figure 19 summarizes some of the ways to have a good conversation.

Ways to Have a Good Comprehension Conversation

▶ Be sure you have read and thought about the information in the book. If you know the text well, you can better discuss it. (The *benchmark books* text characteristics in *Appendix A* will help here.)

▶ Read the key understandings and prompts prior to the assessment so you are very familiar with them.

▶ Tell students that you are going to meet with each one of them to listen to them read so you will be able to help them as readers. Explain that you will ask them to read a short book and then you want them to tell all their thinking about what they read. Sometimes you will ask questions to help them talk more about the book, but you want them to do as much talking about the book as they can.

▶ Invite the student to share thinking and be sure to leave some silence before jumping in. It is very important to provide enough "wait time" for students, especially English language learners, to muster their thoughts and put them into words.

▶ Rephrase comments or prompt questions to be sure the student understands.

▶ Use open-ended probes such as "tell more," "say more," "why?" or "what else?"

▶ Think of different ways to ask the same question or to get the information.

▶ Allow the student to look back in the text if she initiates it. If the student starts to read the book again, stop her by saying, "Just tell about the ideas in your own words."

▶ Use an encouraging tone when inviting the student to talk more.

Figure 19. Ways to have a good comprehension conversation

Figure 20 shows an example of a comprehension conversation about *City Hawks*. The transcript of the conversation is followed by a coded Recording Form reflecting that conversation. Afterwards, we explain the teacher's intentions as she participated in this conversation.

As she initiated this conversation, the teacher was looking for evidence of thinking *within the text* that the student understood and remembered the important information from the text by telling three to four important facts. For example:

▶ A hawk built a nest on a building in New York.

▶ He raised baby birds.

▶ People liked to watch them.

▶ Some people didn't like so many people watching the building.

▶ They took the nest down.

▶ People made them put the nest back.

▶ The graphic on page 4 of *City Hawks* shows that the building is across the street from the park. This is important because Pale Male can hunt for food in the park.

The student does not have to remember every detail of the text. That would not be efficient. If readers are struggling to remember everything, their minds will work only on literal comprehension. They will remember both important and irrelevant details; enjoyment will be decreased and higher level comprehension will suffer. But it is important for them to grasp essential information.

The teacher was also looking for evidence of thinking *beyond the text*—what the reader inferred, connected to prior knowledge, predicted from context, and synthesized new knowledge. For example:

▶ Hawks live in the country, but Pale Male built his nest in the city.

▶ Pale Male built his nest on the building because it was near the park but safe.

▶ People liked to watch Pale Male and his babies because they do not get to see hawks in the city (or other reason consistent with the text).

▶ The nest was removed because people in the building didn't like being watched all the time with binoculars.

▶ Some people liked Pale Male and his nest, and some people didn't like him.

Finally, in the comprehension conversation, the teacher was looking for evidence that the student could think *about the text*. For example:

▶ The writer first gave some information about hawks and then told the story in chronological order.

▶ The writer presented two sides of an argument.

▶ The writer seems to support the idea that the nest should stay on the building.

Figure 21 shows how the teacher scored this conversation.

Comprehension Conversation — *City Hawks*—Level M

Teacher - Student Interaction

Invites conversation.

T: Talk about what happened in the story.

S: There was a hawk. I think his name was Pale Male. He couldn't find a place to build his nest in the country, so he went to a big apartment building and built a nest.

Probes further.

T: What else?

S: He wasn't supposed to have a nest on the building and they took it down—or the stuff it was on, they took it down.

Probes further.

T: Then what happened?

S: They got mad—the people who liked the hawks—and so they had to put it up again.

Asks for information about the end.

T: And what happened at the end?

S: He gets to stay there and build a nest and have baby hawks.

Asks for interpretation of a graphic.

T: Tell what you learned from the drawing on page 4.

S: You can see here that the building is right next to the park, so that's how he found it.

Asks for inference.

T: Why did some people want the nest taken down?

S: They were maybe scared because all those people were looking at them with binoculars. They were really looking at the hawks but also the people who lived there.

Asks for inference.

T: I wonder why they wanted to look at Pale Male and his babies.

S: They don't get to see baby birds because normally he would build the nest in the country. So it was neat to see them.

Asks for comparison.

T: So, what were the two different sides in the argument—the two ways different people felt about Pale Male?

S: Some people liked him and wanted him to stay so they could watch him, but people who lived there didn't want the nest so the crowds would go away.

Probes further.

T: Anything else?

S: Some people like birds but some people don't.

Figure 20. Sample comprehension conversation, *City Hawks*

Continued on next page

Comprehension Conversation — *City Hawks*—Level M

Teacher - Student Interaction

Probes for awareness of text structure.

T: Look at the three sections and read the headings. Do you think this was a good way to organize the information?

S: (Reading) A Nest in the City, Baby Birds, Helping Pale Male. Yes.

T: Why do you think that?

S: It's the different things that happen at different times. First, he builds the nest, and then the babies hatch. And then there is trouble but it turns out okay.

Probes for awareness of compare and contrast.

T: How did the writer help you understand two different points of view about the hawks?

S: She just told why each of them had a good reason for wanting the nest down or wanting it to stay.

Probes for inference.

T: I wonder what side the writer is on.

S: Oh, she likes Pale Male and is glad he can stay. You can tell by the ending where it says he is so famous.

Figure 20. Sample comprehension conversation, *City Hawks*

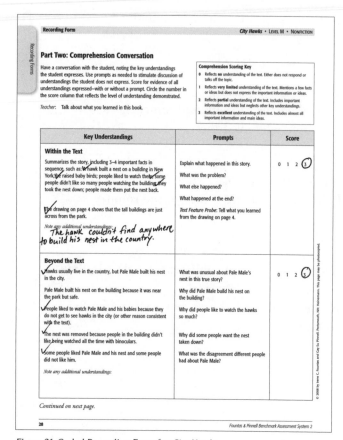

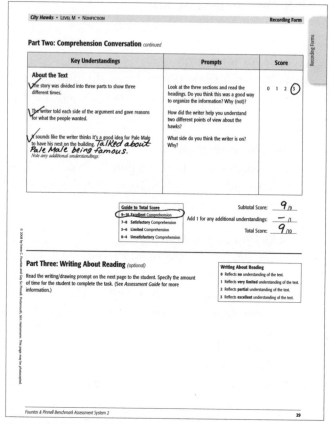

Figure 21. Coded Recording Form for *City Hawks*

Figure 21. Coded Recording Form for *City Hawks*

Selecting Books to Find Easy, Instructional, and Hard Texts for the Student

At this point you should have an accuracy score, a fluency rating, and a comprehension conversation score on the student's reading of at least one benchmark book. Take a look at these three scores.

If you started the assessment on a level that is easy for the reader—that is, one that the student can read fluently with 98–100% accuracy and excellent or satisfactory comprehension (Benchmark Independent level)—give the student a higher level text for the next reading and have the student continue reading more difficult texts until the accuracy rate falls below 95%.

If you started with a hard text, one that a student reads with less than 95% accuracy, you can simply move to a lower level text until you find a text that the student can read independently (98–100% accuracy) with satisfactory or excellent comprehension.

Your goal is to have the student read until you have recorded at least three categories of texts for this student and this time: (1) his Benchmark Independent level (98–100% accuracy with excellent or satisfactory comprehension); (2) his Benchmark Instructional level (95–97% accuracy with excellent or satisfactory comprehension *or* 98–100% accuracy with limited comprehension); and (3) a hard text—the level that's too hard for him to read (below 95% accuracy with any comprehension score). The hard text is important because it defines the instructional level.

Choosing the Writing About Reading Assessment

After you've finished assessing a student's oral reading, you may want to have her write to the prompt in part three of the Recording Form for one of the books she read, ideally for the instructional-level text. The writing is an optional part of the assessment. It provides additional evidence of the reader's understanding and a concrete sample of thinking that can go in the student's folder. The writing assessment is best completed immediately after the comprehension conversation, but the instructional-level text may not be the last one the student read. Allow her to look back at the book, but make sure she understands that she should write in her own words, not copy from the book. Figure 22 is an example of Shreya's writing about an advanced text, *Surviving the Blitz*.

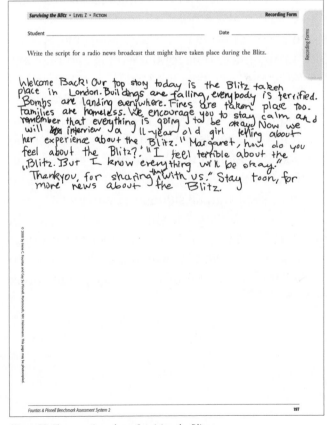

Figure 22. Shreya writes about *Surviving the Blitz*

Shreya was asked to take the point of view of a newscaster in writing about the Blitz. Notice that she not only reported on the devastation but also worked in an interview with the young girl writing the memoir.

Some students perform better if they have a chance to reflect and think about the text in the process of sketching and/or writing. They may reveal in writing greater understanding than they do in the initial conversation. On the other hand, some students have far better ability to talk about a text than to write about it. If the student has only sketched a picture, invite him to tell about it while you record the ideas. You will find that the writing prompt provides a very useful opportunity for your students to share their thinking through writing in a way similar to that required in many standardized tests.

Read the directions to the student and answer any questions he may have. All of the Writing About Reading assessments include the option of sketching or drawing. You will want to help students understand that they should make a quick sketch, not engage in a detailed drawing that takes a long time. Specify an amount of time for the writing and drawing. At levels L–Q, give the student a maximum of twenty minutes. Levels R–U may require a little more time; and levels V–Z may require up to thirty minutes (see Figure 23). If you choose to specify different maximum time limits for each level of the writing assessment, be sure to be consistent with all students at the level.

While writing, the student may look back in the text and may refer to examples from the text but should use his own words. Remember to tell the student, "You can look back at the book

Text Level	Recommended Maximum Time for Writing About Reading
L–Q	Twenty minutes
R–U	Twenty-five minutes
V–Z	Thirty minutes

Figure 23. Recommended writing about reading time

to check your ideas, but you need to tell your thinking in your own words." If you are working in the classroom, the student can complete this assignment as independent work, but you may want to ask him to work quietly at a location near you—but not so near that he can hear the content of your conversation. This will allow you to control the time he spends on the task and to ensure concentration. While one student is working on the written response, you can begin assessing the next student on your list or complete the scoring on the Recording Form.

Continuing the Benchmark Assessment Conference

You have learned how to administer, code, and score a student's reading of one benchmark book. To complete the assessment conference, you want to gather more information about the student's ability to read easy, instructional, and hard texts. Your goal is to determine how the student reads all three types of text. The hard and easy texts help you identify the instructional text. You can use Figure 24 to help you find all three types of text to conclude the assessment conference.

Finding Easy, Instructional, and Hard Texts	
If the first book is...	**Then...**
Easy Student reads at 98–100% accuracy with excellent or satisfactory comprehension.	Move to a higher level text and repeat the same process until the student reads a text that is hard.
Instructional Student reads at 95–97% accuracy with excellent or satisfactory comprehension *or* 98–100% accuracy with limited comprehension.	Move to a lower level text and repeat the same process until the student reads a text that is easy; then move to a higher level text until the student reads a text that is hard.
Hard Student reads at below 95% accuracy with any score on comprehension.	Move to a lower level text and repeat the same process until the student reads a text at an instructional level; then move to a lower level until the student reads a text that is easy.

Figure 24. Finding easy, instructional, and hard texts

Completing the Scoring on Each Recording Form

Before compiling the results of the Benchmark Assessment on the Assessment Summary form, you will want to complete scoring you may not have done during administration (see Figure 25). You should already have an oral reading accuracy rate, a general evaluation of fluency, and a comprehension conversation score. Calculating the number of self-corrections and reading rate (and Writing About Reading if you chose to assign it), will provide additional information for decision making.

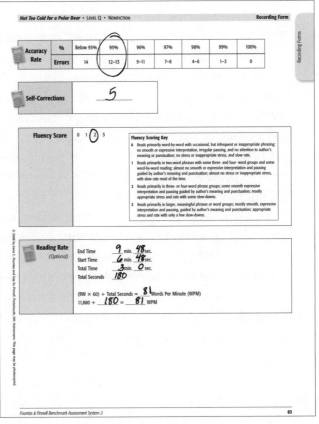

Figure 25. Oral reading score page for *Not Too Cold for a Polar Bear*

Counting the Number of Self-Corrections

The self-correction number quantifies the extent to which the student is monitoring or noticing errors in his own reading.

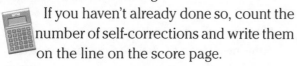 If you haven't already done so, count the number of self-corrections and write them on the line on the score page.

Calculating Reading Rate

Reading rate is a measure of how many words per minutes a student reads. Rate is important because it is one indicator of the reader's ability to process with ease. When the reader processes the print at a satisfactory pace, he is more likely to be able to attend to the meaning of the text. He is also more likely to group words as they are naturally spoken instead of reading one word at a time. It is possible for a reader to read individual words—one at a time—quickly, so it will be important for you to notice speed along with the other dimensions of fluency. Phrasing, or grouping words, is critical to effective processing of the text.

If you use the F & P Calculator/Stopwatch to time the reading, you need only enter the number of running words (RW) from the front cover of the benchmark book. The calculator will give you the words per minute (WPM) to record on the Recording Form. If you use a clock or stopwatch, figure the total reading time in seconds and divide this into the number provided on the Recording Form to get the number of WPM.

Readers will develop individual styles for oral reading, so do not try to identify a precise reading rate that all must achieve. Use the chart in Figure 26 only to identify whether a student's reading is within a desired range. It may also help to think about the range of reading rate you want by the end of the grade level. Remember

that rate is a good indicator only if the student is reading a text that is not too difficult. On hard texts, all readers will read more slowly. Also, be sure to remember that all the dimensions of fluent reading (see page 28) are as important as rate. Reading rate is only one aspect of integrated and orchestrated processing of text.

End of Grade	Oral Reading Rates (WPM)
3 (L–P)	80–120
4 (O–T)	100–140
5 (S–W)	120–160
6 (V–Y)	140–180
7/8 (X–Z)	160–220

Figure 26. Expected oral reading rates at grade and instructional levels

Scoring the Writing About Reading Assessment

After the student has finished writing about reading, collect it for scoring. The purpose of this writing is to examine it for evidence of the student's understanding of the instructional-level text, so you will not be scoring it for conventions or craft, although you may want to notice the student's use of these. Look at the ideas that the writing reflects and assign a score using the guide shown in Figure 27. The Writing About Reading scoring key on your Recording Form is an abbreviated version of this rubric.

When Jan wrote about *Not Too Cold for a Polar Bear,* her writing reflected excellent understanding of the text (see Figure 28), so the teacher gave it a score of 3.

Scoring Key		Rubric
0	Reflects **no** understanding of the text	The writing is not connected with text or is connected only in a very peripheral way (for example, about the same topic). The student's writing does not reflect any of the information in the text (thinking within the text) or of thinking beyond or about the text.
1	Reflects **very limited** understanding of the text	The writing is connected with the text but reveals either very little understanding or confusion. The student's writing does not reflect thinking beyond or about the text.
2	Reflects **partial** understanding of the text	The writing provides evidence that the student understands the literal meaning of the text (within), including key understandings, and in addition, is thinking beyond the text. It is not necessary for the writing to "retell" the text, but examples from it may be used as evidence.
3	Reflects **excellent** understanding of the text	The writing provides evidence that the student not only understands the literal meaning of the text (within) but grasps the author's message and is thinking beyond and about the text. It is not necessary for the writing to "retell" the text, but summaries, quotes, or examples may be offered in support of points.

Figure 27. Rubric for scoring writing about reading

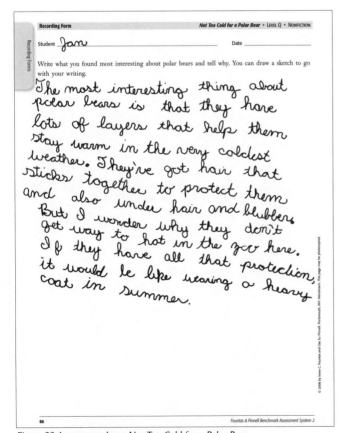

Figure 28. Jan wrote about *Not Too Cold for a Polar Bear*

Choosing Optional Assessments

If your district requires particular assessments in the areas of phonics, word analysis, or vocabulary, the *Assessment Forms* book and CD-ROM provide a variety of optional assessments from which to choose depending on the local need. See Appendix B for a complete list of these assessments. In addition, a student's previous records or his oral reading performance on the Benchmark Assessment may suggest areas you want to explore further. A High Frequency Word assessment, for example, may confirm your hypothesis that a reader's fluency is due to her lack of automatic recognition of high frequency words. A Vocabulary-in-Context assessment will provide insight into a reader's use of meaning cues.

Analyzing and Interpreting Results of the
Fountas & Pinnell Benchmark Assessment System

In this section, you will find step-by-step instructions for using the Assessment Summary form to compile assessment results as well as guidance in determining implications for instruction. You'll be filling out an Assessment Summary form for each reader you have assessed.

The Assessment Summary form is a summary record of key information from each of the individual Recording Forms you used with a student. It includes results from multiple Recording Forms and so provides an overall snapshot of a student's reading at one point in time and summarizes the Benchmark Assessment conference. Information from the Assessment Summary can be entered into the *Data Management* CD-ROM for individual and group data analysis and reporting. The first two pages of the section present a walk-through of the form. A detailed explanation follows.

Assessment Summary Walk-Through

The Assessment Summary form contains

6 A benchmark results box at the top of the page to record the two Benchmark levels you checked below and a Recommended Placement level

1 Space at the top for student, grade, date, teacher, and school information

2 A place to list, from easiest to hardest, the titles, genres, and levels of books the student read during the assessment conference

3 Columns for transferring from the Recording Form all scores for the books read (up to five books)

4 Boxes to check for Benchmark Independent and Benchmark Instructional levels. Check the box next to the level that meets the accuracy and comprehension criteria.

5 Space at the bottom to record comments about specific reading behaviors you noticed during the assessment conference or observed in reviewing the scores as well as any instructional implications the assessment data may suggest

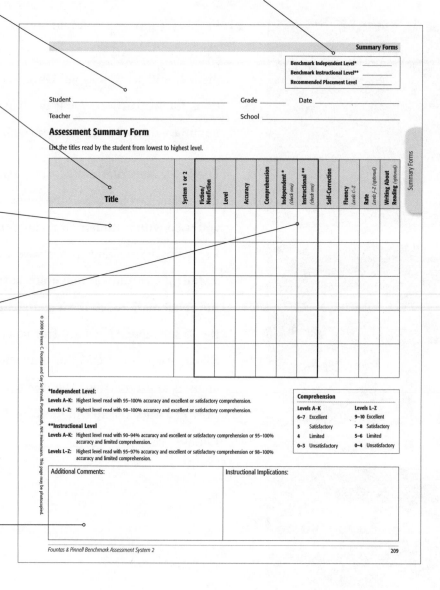

Summary Forms

Benchmark Independent Level* _____
Benchmark Instructional Level** _____
Recommended Placement Level _____

Student _____ Grade _____ Date _____

Teacher _____ School _____

Assessment Summary Form

List the titles read by the student from lowest to highest level.

Title	System 1 or 2	Fiction/ Nonfiction	Level	Accuracy	Comprehension	Independent * (check one)	Instructional ** (check one)	Self-Correction	Fluency Levels C–Z	Rate Levels J–Z (optional)	Writing About Reading (optional)

*Independent Level:
Levels A–K: Highest level read with 95–100% accuracy and excellent or satisfactory comprehension.
Levels L–Z: Highest level read with 98–100% accuracy and excellent or satisfactory comprehension.

**Instructional Level
Levels A–K: Highest level read with 90–94% accuracy and excellent or satisfactory comprehension or 95–100% accuracy and limited comprehension.
Levels L–Z: Highest level read with 95–97% accuracy and excellent or satisfactory comprehension or 98–100% accuracy and limited comprehension.

Comprehension

Levels A–K		Levels L–Z	
6–7	Excellent	9–10	Excellent
5	Satisfactory	7–8	Satisfactory
4	Limited	5–6	Limited
0–3	Unsatisfactory	0–4	Unsatisfactory

Additional Comments:

Instructional Implications:

© 2008 by Irene C. Fountas and Gay Su Pinnell. Portsmouth, NH: Heinemann. This page may be photocopied.

Fountas & Pinnell Benchmark Assessment System 2

209

Benchmark Independent Level

The **Benchmark Independent** level is the highest level at which a student can read independently. The benchmark texts at this level are "easy" for the student. The student can read 98–100% of the words accurately with excellent or satisfactory comprehension.

Benchmark Instructional Level

The **Benchmark Instructional** level is the highest level at which a student can read with good opportunities for learning through teaching. For the level to be instructional, one of the following should be true:

▶ The student can read 95–97% of the words accurately with satisfactory or excellent comprehension.

▶ The student can read 98–100% of the words accurately with limited comprehension.

In both cases, word solving is sufficient. In the second case, word solving is excellent but the student needs instruction to help him understand the texts at the level.

Recommended Placement Level

The **Recommended Placement** level is the level you decide is appropriate for reading instruction. It reflects your thinking about all of the data gathered during the assessment. Most of the time, this level will be the same as the benchmark instructional level, but sometimes a look at the reading behaviors and the specific data will lead you to a different decision.

Filling Out the Assessment Summary Form

Fill out an Assessment Summary form for each reader you have assessed. For each student, fill out the information at the top of the Assessment Summary form and organize the Recording Forms for the books she read in the order of book level from lowest to highest text level. List the book titles, genres, and levels on the Assessment Summary form in this order. Then transfer from the Recording Forms to the Assessment Summary form the accuracy rate, comprehension score, and any other data you have figured on the reading of each book (Figure 29).

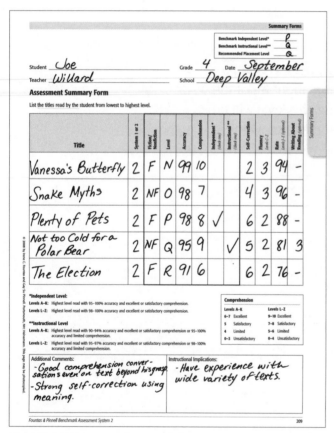

Figure 29. Joe's Assessment Summary form

Finding Three Levels

Altogether, you will determine three different levels for each of your students: a Benchmark Independent level, a Benchmark Instructional level, and a Recommended Placement level. The first two are determined by the accuracy and comprehension scores you have already recorded. The third is determined by your careful analysis of the numbers and the quality of the student's processing.

First, look at the accuracy and comprehension scores you have recorded on the Assessment Summary form. Check the independent column next to the highest level at which a student can read 98–100% of the words accurately with excellent or satisfactory comprehension. Check the instructional column next to the highest level at which a student can read 95–97% of the words accurately with excellent or satisfactory comprehension *or* the highest level at which the student reads 98–100% of the words accurately with limited comprehension. A reading with unsatisfactory comprehension cannot be the instructional level. An accuracy score below 95% cannot be the instructional level.

The table in Figure 30 provides a quick summary of the criteria for Benchmark Independent-level and Benchmark Instructional-level identification.

Finding the Recommended Placement level requires considering and interpreting these scores as well as looking across the rich range of information you gain from a benchmark assessment. In fact, no matter what the test is like, it always requires qualitative judgment on the part of a teacher. When you finish the benchmark assessment for an individual, you have an important set of numbers: (1) a percentage of words read accurately and (2) a comprehension score. You also have additional information on the reader's

▶ fluency in oral reading

▶ use of sources of information

▶ oral reading behaviors (errors, substitutions, self-corrections), or the way the reader processed the text

▶ ability to write about the meaning of the text

You can draw on all of these sources of information to help you look beyond the numbers to make a decision about a student's Recommended Placement level. The Recommended Placement level may be the same as the Benchmark Instructional level, but it may differ because of other factors that come out of your analysis. Look again at the accuracy and comprehension scores. Think beyond the categories and numbers you considered for benchmark levels to make a good decision regarding placement at a level for small-group instruction.

Following are some general factors to think about when using data to select a recommended placement level for a student.

Actual Scores

Look at the *actual* scores rather than the categories only. While we have to establish "cut-offs" for logistic reasons, consider how close to the cutoff point a reader is. In real terms, there really is very little difference between 94 and 95%. However, it does make a difference whether the accuracy rate is 90 or 50% or whether the comprehension score is 4 or 0.

These scores can make big differences and can figure into your placement decisions.

Fluency and Phrasing

Look at the student's fluency and phrasing. Some students read accurately but very slowly; slow reading generally interferes with comprehension. On the other hand, students may read fluently but carelessly, making many errors and losing comprehension. If a student reads a text at 95% accuracy but very slowly with almost no phrasing or recognition of the punctuation, then meaning will be affected. This kind of pattern suggests that you should teach intensively for fluency and phrasing at that level. Or you can move to an easier level for a short time if the other data indicate the level is too difficult for the student.

Text Content

Look at the content of the material. The student's background experience is a critical factor in comprehension. If a student has a great deal of background in an area, she may be able to answer questions or talk about the content even if the text is hard, so the comprehension score may be artificially high. Conversely, if the student lacks background knowledge or does not understand the culture represented in the text, her scores may be artificially low. The student may or may not be able to read other books at the level.

Accuracy	Comprehension			
	Excellent 9–10	**Satisfactory** 7–8	**Limited** 5–6	**Unsatisfactory** 0–4
98–100%	Independent	Independent	Instructional	Hard
95–97%	Instructional	Instructional	Hard	Hard
Below 95%	Hard	Hard	Hard	Hard

Figure 30. Finding the benchmark levels

Sources of Information

Take a quick look at sources of information the reader used as she read the text: meaning (M), language structure (S), and visual information (V). As you analyze errors and self-corrections, you can make hypotheses about the extent to which a reader is using different sources of information. For example, a student might read a text with 95% accuracy but make substitutions that indicate use of the first letter of a word only without evidence of trying to make sense of a text. Another student might read the same text with 92% accuracy but show effective use of word analysis strategies and good comprehension.

Problem-Solving Actions

Look at the reader's use of processing strategies or problem-solving actions. Notice if the reader makes several attempts or notices and corrects errors independently. Notice if the reader has a variety of ways to solve words. Think about whether these actions are effective and efficient. Some repeated errors signal a lack of self-monitoring, but they also can make the accuracy percentage artificially low.

Level of Independence

Look at the reader's independence in problem solving while reading the text. It makes a difference whether the student is actively problem solving or simply waiting to be told a word. For example, a student might read a text with 95% accuracy but stop and appeal at every unfamiliar word. This student is not demonstrating the ability to take risks and to actively search for and use information to solve words.

To make this decision-making process clearer, we provide examples and explanations of how additional considerations might influence Recommended Placement levels (Figures 31–33).

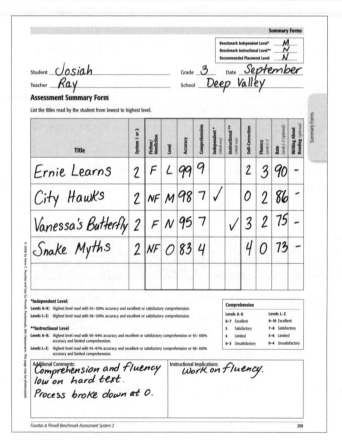

Figure 31. From Josiah's Assessment Summary form

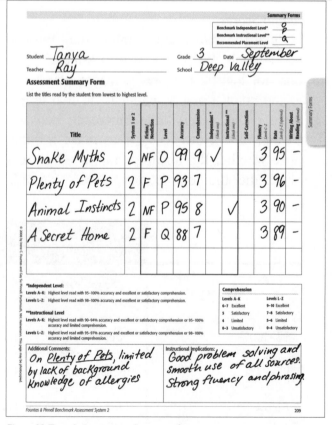

Figure 32. Tanya's Assessment Summary form

Josiah's benchmark scores (Figure 31) lead directly to his placement level. They fall neatly within the expected ranges, and the Recommended Placement level matches the Instructional level of N. The teacher would realize, however, that Josiah needs very supportive teaching to effectively process level N. His accuracy and comprehension are both borderline, and his processing broke down at level O.

Although Tanya's benchmark scores (Figure 32) suggest that she should be placed at level P, other factors contribute to Ms. Ray's decision for a higher placement at level Q. When Tanya read the level P fiction text, her accuracy was 93% and her comprehension was satisfactory despite the fact that she understood little about the sources of allergies. So Ms. Ray had her read the nonfiction text. This time, her accuracy was in the instructional range and comprehension was excellent. Ms. Ray had her read the level Q fiction text and, again, her comprehen-

sion was excellent. Ms. Ray was confident that Tanya could read level Q with good teaching support.

Kaitlin's benchmark scores (Figure 33) indicate level T placement, but her teacher has a rationale for placing her at level S. Kaitlin's Benchmark Instructional level is T but her teacher noted that her Benchmark Independent level was borderline (98% accuracy with low excellent comprehension). Her teacher decided to drop down a level for a short time and begin instruction at level S, knowing that Kaitlin would gain fluency and firm up her processing prior to moving to level T.

The box in the upper right corner of the Summary form provides a place to record all three levels. In summary, the levels you determine for each student are shown in Figure 34 on the next page.

Once you determine the student's Recommended Placement level, you can use the information to form guided reading groups and select texts for your lessons. Once you begin instruction and gain more evidence, you can always adjust the students' grouping if a placement is not working well.

Figure 33. Kaitlin's benchmark levels

Determining Three Levels	
Benchmark Independent level	98–100% accuracy with excellent or satisfactory comprehension
Benchmark Instructional level	95–97% accuracy with excellent or satisfactory comprehension, or 98–100% accuracy with limited comprehension
Recommended Placement level	Best level for instruction after considering accuracy, comprehension, fluency, and processing strategies

Figure 34. Determining Benchmark and Recommended Placement levels

Solving Problems When the Numbers Do Not Match Up Perfectly

When you determine Benchmark Independent and Instructional levels, you are considering several variables rather than accuracy alone. It is worth the extra trouble it may take to look in this complex way because some students are extraordinarily competent as word solvers, but they do not think actively enough or they do not have enough background experience to understand what they are reading. There may be figurative language or big ideas that they do not understand. This kind of reading reveals strengths but does not add up to effective processing. In addition, it provides an unreliable view of the reader. A student who is "word calling" without understanding will not be able to function well on tests and will find it hard to learn from reading.

Occasionally, a student will read with low accuracy but be able to respond to questions—either from getting the gist of the story or from previously held background knowledge. This kind of reader may be merely careless about errors or have word solving difficulties that will affect future ability to process harder texts.

Because we have introduced a high criterion for accuracy as well as for comprehension, you may find that occasionally, numbers do not exactly match the criteria for each of these levels. This will not be a problem when you are using the benchmark criteria for your own information and grouping. For example, you can have two independent levels (slightly different from each other) and then a hard text. You would simply make a decision on the placement level based on all the information and record the instructional level as the highest level read before the text was too hard.

However, you may need to report two or three of the levels to the principal or the central office of your district. In this case, we have prepared the chart in Figure 35. Here you will find some cases in which the numbers do not neatly match up. In the third column you will find the teacher's solution to the problem. Find the one that most closely matches your own case and use it to help you make decisions about recording levels.

After you have solved many of these problems, you will find that you can make these decisions quickly.

Finding Benchmark Levels When the Numbers Do Not Match Up Perfectly

Problem	Example of student scores:	Solution
The student has 2+ independent levels and no instructional level.	P at 98% accuracy with excellent comprehension Q at 98% accuracy with satisfactory comprehension R at 93% accuracy with limited comprehension	Take the highest level read independently and make it the placement level. Expect the student to move quickly. P = Independent level Q = Independent level Q = Recommended Placement level Remember that students reading at this level will *always* have many independent levels (all below the instructional level).
The student has 2 instructional levels. *should be placement level*	P at 97% accuracy with excellent comprehension Q at 95% accuracy with satisfactory comprehension R at 95% accuracy with satisfactory comprehension	Take the highest level instructional text P = Instructional level Q = Instructional level Q = Recommended Placement level Expect this student to move quickly to level R as you work on word solving strategies.
The student has no instructional level because the reading is uneven.	M at 98% accuracy with satisfactory comprehension N at 94% accuracy with satisfactory comprehension O at 98% accuracy with satisfactory comprehension P at 90% accuracy with limited comprehension	For instruction, you want to be sure you are on firm ground. With uneven reading like this, select the level you are most sure that the student can process with your help. Monitor placement carefully. M = Independent level N = Hard level O = Independent level P = Hard level N = Recommended Placement level
The student has no instructional level because of very high accuracy on two levels, unsatisfactory comprehension on the next highest level, and low accuracy and unsatisfactory comprehension on the next.	K at 100% accuracy with satisfactory comprehension L at 99% accuracy with satisfactory comprehension M at 98% accuracy with unsatisfactory comprehension N at 75% accuracy with unsatisfactory comprehension	For instruction, use a text that the student can comprehend with your support. Select level L and work on active thinking. You should be able to move quickly to M. K = Independent level L = Instructional level L = Recommended Placement level

Figure 35. Finding the benchmark levels

Continued on next page

Finding the Benchmark Levels When the Numbers Do Not Match Up Perfectly

Problem	Example of student scores	Solution
The reader's comprehension is uneven, with unsatisfactory comprehension at a particular level.	L at 98% accuracy with satisfactory comprehension M at 95% accuracy with unsatisfactory comprehension N at 91% accuracy with satisfactory comprehension	You might want to try the alternate text at level M to see if the particular text had content that was unfamiliar to the student. Select N for instruction, but observe the reader closely and support comprehension. L = Independent level N = Instructional level
You do not have an independent level.	R at 98% accuracy with limited comprehension S at 92% accuracy with limited comprehension	You need to try levels Q and perhaps P to get a level the reader can process with satisfactory comprehension (independent level). R = Instructional level
You do not have an instructional level because there appears to be a large gap between two readings.	Q at 99% accuracy with excellent comprehension R at 85% accuracy with limited comprehension S at 72% accuracy with limited comprehension	R is too hard for instructing this reader, and Q is obviously an easy text. Try the reader on the alternate level R text just to check whether there is a particular difficulty with content. Q = Independent level Q = Instructional level Q = Placement level
		The student may read some books on level P as independent reading. Work to move the student quickly to R for instructional level.
All the texts seem too hard for the reader.	L at 75% accuracy with limited comprehension M at 60% accuracy with limited comprehension N at 55% accuracy with limited comprehension	You need to keep going down in level. If the Benchmark Assessment System 1 is available in your school, switch to that system to try easier texts.
All the texts seem too hard for the reader to understand.	P at 98% accuracy with unsatisfactory comprehension Q at 100% accuracy with unsatisfactory comprehension R at 97% accuracy with unsatisfactory comprehension	You need to keep going down in level until you find a text that the reader can comprehend with limited comprehension (and 98%–100% accuracy) or satisfactory or excellent comprehension (and 95%–97% accuracy).
The student has no instructional level because all levels appear to be easy.	X at 98% accuracy with excellent comprehension Y at 98% accuracy with satisfactory comprehension Z at 98% accuracy with satisfactory comprehension	This is a good problem to have! Just indicate Z as instructional level and Y as independent level. This student will benefit from small group discussion, extending understanding through writing, and wide reading experience. Select age-appropriate material.

Figure 35. Finding the benchmark levels, *continued*

Looking More Closely at Benchmark Text Reading

Now that you have determined the three levels, you know the level to recommend for each student for independent reading and the level at which you will begin instruction. At this point, you will want to examine the Benchmark Assessment results for additional information to inform instruction. We recommend looking carefully at the student's reading of at least one of the assessment conference texts. Choose the reading you feel provides the most information about the reader's text processing. Usually this reading will be the Benchmark Instructional-level text, though you may find some useful data in the independent-level text as well. As you analyze the reading of the text, note the reading behaviors that the student controls, partially controls, or does not yet control. You can also examine the reader's ability to use the sources of information in the text.

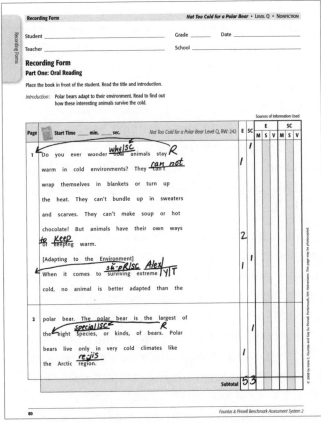

Figure 36. Coded oral reading of *Not Too Cold for a Polar Bear*

Analyzing Sources of Information

To inform teaching, analyze the student's errors and self-corrections on her Benchmark Instructional-level text to find out what kinds of information the reader is using and what kinds of information are being neglected. For example, a reader who consistently makes substitution errors like *whole* for *entire* may be thinking about the meaning of the text but neglecting to check with the letters in the word. A reader who consistently makes errors like *serve* for *survive* may be noticing the letters but neglecting to think about whether the reading sounds right and makes sense. (The *Professional Development* DVD provides support in decision making based on this information.)

After tallying each error and self-correction on the Recording Form (see Figure 36), look at the number and kinds of errors and self-corrections the student has made. Look at the far right sources of information columns. Begin by writing MSV next to each error in the error column. For self-corrections, write MSV in the error column and in the self-correction column. For both the errors (E) and the self-corrections (SC), you are going to hypothesize and record the sources of information that the reader was using when he made the error or self-correction, determining if the student was using meaning (M), structure (S), or visual information (V) at the time (see Figure 37 on the next page).

▶ *Meaning.* Readers often make substitutions that indicate they are thinking about the meaning of the text. For example, a reader might say *ballet* for *dance*. Ask yourself: Did the meaning of the text influence the error? If so, circle the *M* in the sources of information column under error (E).

▶ *Structure.* A powerful source of information for a reader is the structure of language. From our knowledge of oral language, we have implicit understanding of the way words are put together to form phrases and sentences. It "sounds right" to us. Readers often substitute nouns for nouns or verbs for verbs, indicating an awareness of the structure of language. For example, a reader might say *I imagine we two sitting across a table* for *I imagine that the two of us are sitting across a table.* The reader has made several errors in reading one sentence but moves right on. For each error, ask yourself: Does the error fit an acceptable English language structure? Did structure influence the error? If so, circle the *S* in the sources of information column under error (E).

Note: Readers often use multiple sources of information as they process texts. You might code some of these errors as both *S* (the student

substituted one verb construction for another) and *M*. Not self-correcting these relatively minor errors might make sense in terms of efficiency; however, it signals that the reader is neglecting visual information, which may lead to loss of meaning at other places in the text.

▶ *Visual information.* Readers use the visual features of print—the letters and words—to read. They connect these features to phonetic information that exists in their heads. For example, looking at the picture, a reader might say *serve* for *survive*. Ask yourself: Did the visual information from the print influence the error (letter, part, word)? If so, circle *V* in the error column.

▶ *Using sources of information in combination.* Sometimes readers sample only some of the visual information in a word, for example, reading *porch* for *podium* in the sentence: "Later that morning, Jill walked slowly across the auditorium stage and stood behind the podium." A reader who makes this kind of error may not be looking beyond the first letter of the word. Only one error has been made, and in this case the reader might comprehend the text despite the error. But perpetuating this kind of error will inevitably lead to loss of comprehension. *Something* should trigger the reader to notice a mismatch, and it could be the combined knowledge that "something doesn't make sense here" and "*porch* doesn't match the last part of the word."

Use a similar procedure for coding the reader's self-corrections. Here, you are hypothesizing the additional information that the reader might have used to correct the error. The self-correction of course indicates use of all three sources of information—meaning, language structure, and visual information—because it is the accurate word. But you are searching here for what the reader might have used as *additional* information to correct the error.

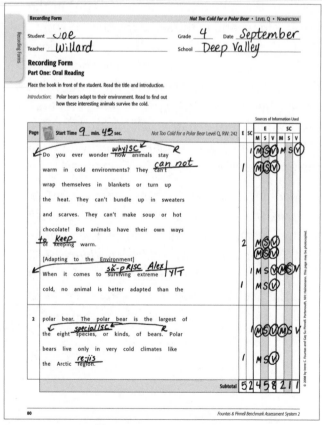

Figure 37. Analyzing errors for sources of information

If the reader made the error *ballet* for *dance*, for example, and then self-corrected, the error would be analyzed as *M,* and in the self-correction column you would circle *S* and *V,* because the reader might have thought about the way the language sounded and might have noticed the *d* or another part of the word. If the reader said *porch* for *podium* and then self-corrected, you would circle *M* in the self-correction column, because the meaning of the text likely influenced the correction.

These analyses will help you look qualitatively at the reader's use of these different sources of information. Think about what the reader is neglecting. You can help the reader attend to the information sources needed as you listen to him read orally during reading lessons or do some teaching after the reading. If readers in a group are neglecting to think about what might make sense, you can prompt them to do so. If they are not noticing the first letter or other part of a word that would be helpful, you can draw the visual information to their attention.

Noting Strategic Actions

Look again at the errors you have marked on the text in the Recording Form for the reader's Benchmark Instructional-level book. Think about the reader as a problem solver. Noting problem areas will be helpful in your thinking:

▶ *Detecting errors.* Rather than reading along and ignoring errors, you want the reader to notice when something doesn't fit. Effective readers are constantly monitoring their own reading accuracy. If the reader does not show signs of checking on himself or self-monitoring, you can draw attention to mismatches and show him how to fix them.

▶ *Self-correcting.* Self-correction is a sign that the reader is monitoring his reading and working actively to make everything fit— meaning, structure, visual information, and the way the reading sounds. You can prompt for self-correction.

▶ *Searching for and using information.* Effective readers actively search for the information they need to read with accuracy, fluency, and understanding. They make attempts that, even if not right, show you they are trying out what they know. You can teach the reader many ways to search for and use multiple sources of information in the text. For nonfiction texts, searching for and using information very often includes using text features such as table of contents, glossary, and headings. Readers are also expected to interpret graphics such as labeled photographs and drawings, maps, diagrams, and charts.

▶ *Solving words.* You want readers to have and use many ways to solve words. As they learn more, they will recognize many words automatically, but they also need to be able to use phonics and word analysis strategies so that they can learn many more. Then you can teach the reader many different ways to solve words.

▶ *Maintaining fluency.* Effective readers put all sources of information together so that their reading sounds fluent and expressive. They read in word groups and stop at punctuation; they stress words in bold and italic type in fiction texts. You can think about how the reading sounded. If the reader is not fluent and the text is easy enough, you can demonstrate fluent reading and show the reader how to put words together so that it sounds good, reading with intonation and logical word groupings.

The set of questions in Figure 39 will be helpful in guiding your thinking as you look at your coding and think about the reading behaviors you observed. This guide can be copied or printed from the *Assessment Forms* book or CD-ROM for easy reference. The questions will help you focus on the actions the reader takes and give you insight into how the reader uses different kinds of information and problem solves his way through the text. You will be able to notice effective and ineffective processing and listen for the reader's ability to maintain fluency. By using the guide regularly, you can train yourself to look beyond the numbers to the reading behaviors that will provide critical information for your teaching.

In Figure 39, notice how Mrs. Willard has used the guide to note important behaviors that Joe evidenced in his reading of *Not Too Cold for a Polar Bear*.

Using this as your guide, make notes on your Assessment Summary form in the boxes labeled "Additional Comments" and "Instructional Implications" (see Figure 38). Your observations of the processing or problem-solving actions the reader is able to use will have important implications for the instruction you provide in your lessons.

Once you have completed an Assessment Summary, you can enter the data into the *Data Management* CD-ROM. Doing so will allow you to track progress over time, analyze trends in reading performance, and compare data within your class in order to inform your instructional plans. After you review and analyze the scores and the strategic actions, note your thinking about areas of the reading process that have important instructional implications. See the following section, "Connecting Benchmark Assessment Results to Instruction," for a summary of ways the assessment can inform instruction.

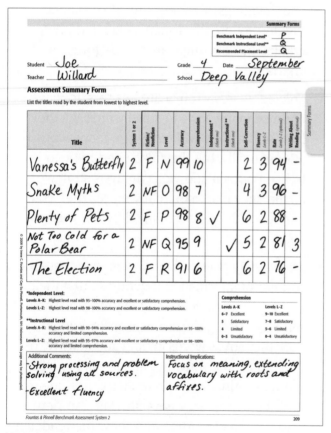

Figure 38. Joe's Assessment Summary form

Expanding Performance Evidence or Diagnosis with Optional Assessments

The extensive information gathered through the basic Benchmark Assessment procedures outlined above provides clear direction for instruction, but you may also wish to get more diagnostic evidence about the student's literacy knowledge through the optional assessments found in the *Assessment Forms* book and CD-ROM (see Appendix B). A Reading Interview, an array of Phonics and Word Analysis Assessments, and a variety of Vocabulary Assessments will provide targeted information about the learner's knowledge in specific areas of literacy learning.

Resources

Name: *Joe*   Date: *September*

Guide for Observing and Noting Reading Behaviors	Notes
1. Attention to Print Features *Does the reader:* • Move left to right across a line of print? • Return to the left for a new line? • Match word by word while reading a line or more of print? • Recognize a few easy high frequency words?	
2. Detecting Errors *Does the reader:* • Hesitate at an unknown word? • Stop at an unknown word? • Stop at an unknown word and appeal for help? • Stop after an error? • Notice mismatches? • Notice when an attempt does not look right? • Notice when an attempt does not sound right? • Notice when an attempt does not make sense? • Reread to confirm reading? • Use knowledge of some high frequency words to check on reading? • Check one source of information with another? • Check an attempt that makes sense with language? • Check an attempt that makes sense with the letters (visual information)? • Use language structure to check on reading? • Request help after making several attempts?	*Usually stops at error or after reading over the error.* *Good repertoire of high frequency words.* *Notices mismatch with visual information.* *Makes attempts that indicate use of visual information.*
3. Self-Correcting *Does the reader:* • Reread and try again until accurate? • Stop after an error and make another attempt? • Stop after an error and make multiple attempts until accurate? • Reread to self-correct? • Work actively to solve mismatches? • Self-correct errors some of the time? • Self-correct errors most of the time?	*Rereads to try again and often self corrects.* *Self corrects about half of the time.*
4. Searching for and Using Information **Meaning** *Does the reader:* • Make meaningful attempts at unknown words? • Use the meaning of the story or text to predict unknown words? • Reread to gather more information to solve a word? • Reread and use the meaning of the sentence? • Reread to search for more details—information, characters, plot? • Reread to gather information to clarify confusions? • Use headings and titles to think about the meaning of a section of text? • Use information in the pictures to help in understanding a text? • Use knowledge of the genre (and its characteristics) to help in understanding a text? • Use knowledge of the genre (and its characteristics) to help in finding information? • Use readers' tools to help in finding information (glossary, index)? **Structure** *Does the reader:* • Use knowledge of oral language to solve unknown words? • Reread to see if a word "sounds right" in a sentence? • Reread to correct using language structure?	*Makes attempt before appealing.* *Rereads to get more info. to solve words.* *Uses headings.* *Can gain info. from drawings and diagrams.* *Rereads to self correct language structure.*

Resources

Figure 39. Guide for observing and noting reading behaviors

continued on next page

© 2008 by Irene C. Fountas and Gay Su Pinnell. Portsmouth, NH: Heinemann. This page may be photocopied.

Guide for Observing . . . (cont.)	Notes
Visual Information *Does the reader:* • Use the visual information to solve words? • Use the sound of the first letter(s) to attempt or solve a word? • Use some, most, or all of the visual information to solve words? • Use sound analysis to solve a word? • Make attempts that are visually similar? • Use knowledge of a high frequency word to problem solve? • Search for more visual information within a word to solve it? • Use analogy to solve unknown words? • Use syllables to solve words? • Use prefixes and suffixes to take apart and recognize words? • Use inflectional endings to problem solve words? • Recognize most words quickly and easily? • Reread and use the sound of the first letter to solve a word? • Problem solve unknown words quickly and efficiently? • Work actively to solve words? • Use two or three sources of information together in attempts at words? • Use all sources of information flexibly to solve words? • Use all sources of information in an orchestrated way?	*Uses all sources needs to keep more attention on meaning and use his vocabulary.*
5. Solving Words *Does the reader:* • Recognize a core of high frequency words quickly? • Recognize most words quickly and easily? • Use a variety of flexible ways to take words apart? • Use the meaning of the sentences to solve words? • Use the structure of the sentence to solve words? • Use some of the visual information to solve words? • Use known word parts to solve words? • Use sound analysis (sounding out)? • Use analogy to solve words? • Make attempts that are visually similar? • Use the sound of the first letter to solve words? • Work actively to solve words? • Use known words or parts to solve unknown words? • Use syllables to problem solve? • Use prefixes and suffixes to take words apart? • Use inflectional endings to take words apart? • Use sentence context to derive the meaning of words? • Use base words and root words to derive the meaning of words? • Make connections among words to understand their meaning?	*Needs to work on using base words and prefixes and suffixes. Also to look at all syllables of words.*
6. Maintaining Fluency *Does the reader:* • Read without pointing? • Read word groups (phrases)? • Put words together? • Read smoothly? • Read the punctuation? • Make the voice go down at periods? • Make the voice go up at question marks? • Pause briefly at commas, dashes, and hyphens? • Read dialogue with intonation or expression? • Stress the appropriate words to convey accurate meaning? • Read at a good rate—not too fast and not too slow?	*Reads ending punctuation-shows in pause and rising or falling intonation. Rate - excellent.*
7. Other	

Resources

Figure 39. Guide for observing and noting reading behaviors

Connecting Benchmark Assessment Results to Instruction

In our view, the most important use of assessment is to inform instruction. Even while administering and analyzing the benchmark conference, you will find yourself thinking about what the student needs in terms of instruction. When you have completed the assessment, you will have valuable categories of information that will allow you to link your findings directly with instruction.

In this section, we discuss and provide models for using assessment results to place students in groups; to plan for individual, small-group, and whole-class instruction; and to use *The Continuum of Literacy Learning* to connect assessment and instruction.

Grouping Students for Instruction

The three levels (Benchmark Independent, Benchmark Instructional, and Recommended Placement) you determined will help you form groups for reading instruction (see Figures 40 and 41). List your students on the Class Record form from lowest to highest instructional level to help you cluster students appropriately. The *Data Management* CD-ROM will allow you to sort a class roster by benchmark level (or other variable), which can assist with instructional groupings.

With the wide range of students in every classroom, it is a challenge to form reading groups that will work efficiently. Ideally, you would have a group for each level, but for the class below, that would mean too many groups. It would take so much time to teach the groups that students would not get reading instruction often enough. Also, there are slight differences in students' processing systems even if they are reading at about the same text level.

As you look at the list, you can see that the teacher has recommended a placement level of P for Diana even though her Benchmark Instructional level is Q. Diana was not fluent at level Q, and the teacher thought she could benefit from more reading at P. Beth's scores did not show her reading at an instructional level V, but the teacher's assessment is that Beth is a more advanced reader than this assessment shows. The teacher plans to do further assessment but is not at all worried about Beth's ability to read and understand texts at V.

Mr. Mason used all the data to make his grouping decisions. Sometimes he clustered students who were at slightly different levels together in the same group. On this Class Record form, you can see that he grouped Sarah, Diana, Troy, and Farah together. Mr. Mason knows that these students need a great deal of help, so he will work with them daily in a small group, starting at P.

Because Farah's comprehension and fluency are strong, Mr. Mason is predicting that she may move to the group with Lisa, Jonathon, David, Kara, Julian, Jennifer, Auggie, Jack, and Jordan before long. He will start this group at R, and

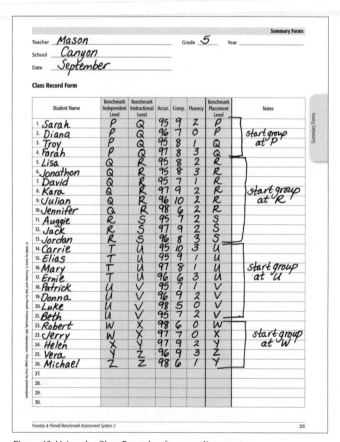

Figure 40. Using the Class Record to form reading groups

Sample Grouping for a Grade 5 Class				
Group	Sarah Diana Troy Farah	Lisa Jonathon David Kara Julian Jennifer Auggie Jack Jordan	Carrie Elias Mary Ernie Patrick Donna Luke Beth	Robert Jerry Helen Vera Michael
Comments	Need daily intensive instruction because they are well below grade level. Observe Farah for possible shift to R.	Give extra challenge to Jack and Jordan.	Give more support to Carrie. Work on fluency.	Search for texts that will challenge the group but be age-appropriate. Avoid texts with issues that are too mature.
Starting level	Start at P.	Start at R and move quickly to S.	Start at U and move quickly to V.	Read age-appropriate texts of interest at W and move to X.

Figure 41. Sample grouping notes for grade 5 class

his agenda will include deep discussion of the texts they are reading as well as some readers' theater to help them with fluency.

Carrie, Elias, Mary, Ernie, Patrick, Donna, Luke, and Beth form a group with a starting point of level U. Luke was not fluent at level V and it seemed difficult for him. The group with Robert, Jerry, Helen, Vera, and Michael will start at W. These six students compose a high-progress group. They read well above grade level but the teacher will take care in selecting texts for them. They need interesting, age-appropriate material. Technically, each could read adult-level literature, but the mature themes and issues might be difficult for them to understand. They need to read widely across genres so that they are engaged in reading interesting texts.

In Figure 41, you can see the five reading groups Mr. Mason has formed, along with his comments.

Benchmark assessment and ongoing assessment allow you to group dynamically as students develop differently from each other. Dynamic grouping means that you move students from group to group as they progress at different rates. You will adjust your groupings as needed. Small, homogeneous groups will enable you to choose appropriate texts and teach closely to the needs of the individual students.

We do not recommend naming the groups so that they have permanent status. Just call the group by the students' names or by the book they read last and invite them to come to the reading table. Also, you will want to have students work in other kinds of groups (for example, literacy work groups or

Individual Instruction	
Data from Benchmark Assessment	**How the Information Helps in Making Teaching Decisions in Literacy Contexts**
▷ Benchmark Independent level ▷ Benchmark Instructional level ▷ Recommended Placement level	▷ Guiding students' book choices for independent reading ▷ Placing the student in a small group for instruction ▷ Reconsidering grouping decisions regarding the individual ▷ Informing individual reading conferences
▷ Evidence of processing (strategic actions and MSV analysis)	▷ Interacting with individuals in guided reading lessons ▷ Interacting with individuals in conferences
▷ Fluency score	▷ Interacting with individuals in guided reading or small-group lessons ▷ Interacting in individual conferences during reading workshop ▷ Determining the need for readers' theater
▷ Comprehension category scores and total score	▷ Interacting with individuals during guided reading or small-group lessons ▷ Interacting with individuals in reading conferences ▷ Responding to writing about reading in the reader's notebook

Figure 42. Benchmark scores and teaching decisions for individuals

heterogeneous literature discussion groups) that are not arranged by reading level. In addition to targeted small-group reading instruction, they will need many other group opportunities for age- and grade-appropriate instruction in interactive read-aloud or shared reading contexts.

Planning Individual, Small-Group, and Whole-Class Instruction

Now let's think about how to use the rich information you collect as you begin working with your students in three instructional contexts: the teaching you do with individuals, small groups, and your entire class (see Figures 42–44).

Individual Instruction

The independent level will help you to guide the students' book choices for productive independent reading. The Benchmark Assessment data are the foundation for placing students in "just right" books for small-group instruction. These levels will also help you think about forming groups of students who, while they are individuals and unique in many ways, are alike enough to teach effectively together. Students learn to read better by reading many texts they *can* read each day. Easy reading has many benefits.

You can gather evidence of processing through analyzing the errors and self-correction behaviors of the student. Use this information to help you as you interact with the student individually during guided reading and read-

Small-Group Instruction	
Data from Benchmark Assessment	**How the Information Helps in Making Teaching Decisions in Literacy Contexts**
▶ Benchmark Independent level ▶ Benchmark Instructional level ▶ Recommended Placement level	▶ Making decisions about grouping ▶ Selecting texts for guided reading or small-group lessons
▶ Evidence of processing (strategic actions and MSV analysis)	▶ Preparing an introduction to the text for a guided reading lesson ▶ Making teaching points in guided reading lessons ▶ Planning word work for the end of the guided reading lesson
▶ Fluency scores	▶ Selecting texts for guided reading or small-group lessons ▶ Making teaching points in guided reading lessons ▶ Selecting ways to reread the text (readers' theater, shared reading)
▶ Comprehension category scores and total score	▶ Introducing texts to students in guided reading lessons ▶ Supporting the student's reading of the text ▶ Discussing the meaning of the text after reading ▶ Making teaching points in guided reading lessons ▶ Extending meaning of a text through writing about reading

Figure 43. Benchmark scores and teaching decisions for small groups

ing conferences. It will also help you to make teaching points in guided reading lessons.

The fluency score and your observation of oral reading will help you know what the student needs in terms of fluency support. It can inform your interactions with the student during guided reading and individual reading conferences. The comprehension category will help you know whether you need to intervene to help the student think more actively before, during, and after reading. Looking at the student's responses in categories (within, beyond, and about texts) will inform your interactions with the student during guided reading and individual conferences.

Small-Group Instruction

The Benchmark Instructional and Recommended Placement levels of your class will help you to form groups and select texts for them to read. Examining the demands of texts at that level will be helpful in constructing introductions to texts before students read them. You can look at the evidence of processing (see Figure 39) for each student, searching for patterns across the group. Chances are, there will be similar needs. Use this information to inform your teaching points after reading.

Whole-Class Instruction	
Data from Benchmark Assessment	**How the Information Helps in Making Teaching Decisions in Literacy Contexts**
▶ Benchmark Independent levels ▶ Benchmark Instructional levels	▶ Stocking the classroom library with books for self-selected independent reading ▶ Giving book talks to students in reading workshop ▶ Providing audio-recorded books for rereading and for literature discussion
▶ Evidence of processing (strategic actions and MSV analysis)	▶ Designing minilessons for reading workshop (strategies and skills) ▶ Engaging students in intentional conversation in interactive read-aloud ▶ Planning word study minilessons ▶ Engaging students in literature discussion
▶ Fluency scores	▶ Engaging students in shared and performance reading ▶ Providing effective models of oral reading through interactive read-aloud
▶ Comprehension category scores and total score	▶ Engaging students in intentional conversation during interactive read-aloud ▶ Engaging students in literature discussion ▶ Providing minilessons (strategies and skills; craft)

Figure 44. Benchmark scores and teaching decisions for whole classes

The fluency scores of individuals in the group help you decide whether to do some intensive teaching or prompt for fluency and phrasing as students read the text. You may want to incorporate readers' theater into your small-group work to help them be more conscious of how their reading sounds.

The comprehension scores will help you know how much you need to support students' active thinking. Of course, you will always be teaching for comprehension because that is one of the main goals of instruction. But you may find that you need to adjust the text level to one that is very accessible and work intensively to get students to express their thinking. Looking at the patterns of performance within categories will help you plan teaching points and design activities for writing about reading that will also extend students' thinking about texts.

Whole-Class Instruction

Individual assessment can inform your teaching of the whole class as well. Use your class list to look at the classroom library. Make sure that you have a quantity of high-quality books at levels your students can read independently. Also, as you make book talks to students, present a range of levels. It is extremely important for students to process a large quantity of text independently every day. You are helping them take on more difficult texts through guided reading instruction, but they also need to be building stamina and skill on their own.

Look across the assessment data for information on processing and comprehension. It's especially important to look at the extent to which students can express their thinking beyond and about texts. This information will be invaluable as you plan minilessons for reading workshop and for intentional conversation during interactive read-aloud. We use the term *intentional conversation* to remind ourselves that we need to simultaneously engage in a real conversation with students and have in mind things that we want to teach them during read-aloud sessions. (See *Teaching for Comprehending and Fluency* [Heinemann, 2006], chapters 15–17, for more description.) Finally, you can use the information to help you extend students' thinking through writing about reading as part of interactive read-aloud and literature discussion.

Connecting Assessment to Instruction with *The Continuum of Literacy Learning*

As you think about individual, small-group, and whole-class instruction, you will find it helpful to consult *The Continuum of Literacy Learning, Grades 3–8: A Guide to Teaching* (Fountas and Pinnell, Heinemann, 2008). This volume contains seven continua (see Figure 45 on page 66). Each continuum focuses on an area of the language arts curriculum. Six continua—Interactive Read-Aloud and Literature Discussion; Shared and Performance Reading; Writing About Reading; Writing; Oral, Visual, and Technological Communication; and Phonics and Word Analysis—provide *grade-level* expectations and are designed for planning group instruction. The seventh, the Guided Reading continuum, is organized by Fountas and Pinnell levels from L to Z and correlates directly with the benchmark levels you arrived at through the Benchmark Assessment. Once you have determined a student's benchmark and placement levels, turn directly to the Guided Reading continuum and find the direct link from the Fountas & Pinnell Benchmark Assessment System to instruction.

(Note: There is also a K–8, A–Z version of the continuum [*The Continuum of Literacy Learning, Grades K–8*], which will be of interest to administrators, curriculum developers, staff developers, and literacy coaches.)

The continua provide specific descriptions of the texts that students read, listen to, write, and perform. In addition, each continuum lists specific behaviors and understandings that are required at each level for students to demonstrate thinking *within*, *beyond*, and *about* the text. Taken together, these behaviors and understandings represent the *demands* of the text. They form what students will be expected to do in order to effectively read and understand the text. The behaviors and understandings are cumulative across the levels. In other words, the reader is taking on new demands as the texts grow more challenging. A student reading level M and successfully meeting the demands of the text is also able to meet the demands of texts on levels A–L.

The Continuum of Literacy Learning, Grades 3–8	
Continuum	**Description**
Guided Reading Levels L–Z	The teacher works with a small group of students who are similar in their development of a reading process. The teacher introduces the text and the students read it with teaching support.
Interactive Read-Aloud and Literature Discussion Grades 3–8	The teacher reads aloud to students and engages them in intentional conversation. Students discuss their thinking in the whole group or in small groups. This continuum also refers to "book clubs," in which students independently read (or listen to) books and then discuss them in small groups. The books are usually organized by the teacher, and students have a limited choice, although they also may be books read aloud.
Shared and Performance Reading Grades 3–8	Students read together (or in parts) a text that they know well. They show with their voices what the text means.
Writing About Reading Grades 3–8	Students respond to reading by writing and sometimes drawing.
Writing Grades 3–8	Students engage in the writing process and produce pieces of their own writing in many genres.
Oral, Visual, and Technological Communication Grades 3–8	Oral language is used across the curriculum and is embedded in all contexts in the continuum. In this continuum, specific expectations are listed and extended to interactive media for communication.
Phonics, Spelling, and Word Study Grades 3–8	A phonics and word study continuum includes expectations related to six areas of learning: letter-sound relationships, high frequency words, word meaning/vocabulary, spelling patterns, word structure, and word-solving actions. The K–8 continuum includes nine areas of learning to cover early understandings such as phonemic awareness.

Figure 45. The Continuum of Literacy Learning, Grades 3–8

Working Step by Step with Benchmark Assessment and the Continuum

Next we provide step-by-step examples for connecting Benchmark Assessments to guided reading, interactive read-aloud, and whole-group reading minilessons in a reading workshop.

Linking Information to Guided Reading Lessons

Step 1. Assess all students in the class and find Benchmark Independent, Benchmark Instructional, and Recommended Placement levels.

Step 2. Form temporary groups according to their placement levels.

Step 3. Go to the Guided Reading continuum and look at the characteristics of the texts at the level. Keep these characteristics in mind when selecting books for the group.

Step 4. Select several possible books for each group so that you will have alternatives across a few days or a week of instruction.

Step 5. Select the text that you will introduce to the group first.

Step 6. Read the text carefully with the characteristics in mind.

Step 7. Look at your student data on strategic actions and sources of information as well as fluency and comprehension. Think about what students need to learn how to do as readers. Reports from the *Data Management* CD-ROM can be helpful in identifying and analyzing patterns.

Step 8. Look at the behaviors and understandings for the level. These represent what students need to be able to do to read successfully at the level.

Step 9. Think about what your students can do and then find behaviors and understandings that they partially control or do not yet control.

Step 10. Plan your introduction to the text and teaching points for the lesson, keeping in mind the processing needs of your students.

Step 11. Plan for word work at the end of the lesson. You will find specific suggestions for each level on the continuum, L–Z. If you have students who need basic work because they are reading well below grade level, you may want to consult the A–N continuum.

Step 12. Plan for writing about reading (optional element). Here, think about the specific demands of text on the Guided Reading continuum. Then, look at the Writing About Reading continuum for the grade level. Look at the genres that are appropriate and the thinking that students are expected to do.

Step 13. As students grow more proficient and reading becomes easy at a particular level, look at the behaviors and understandings for the next highest level. You'll find many of the same strategies you've been teaching because the reading process is built by applying the same set of complex strategies to increasingly more difficult texts. You may find new understandings or more complex versions of the same understandings. Start to look toward this next level.

Step 14. Select texts from the next level and look at the text characteristics and behaviors and understandings to notice, teach, and support.

Step 15. Continue to introduce texts and teach lessons based on the spiraling of text demands.

Linking Assessment Information to Teaching in Interactive Read-Aloud

Step 1. Assess the class and find Benchmark Independent, Benchmark Instructional, and Recommended Placement levels.

Step 2. Look at the total scores for comprehension and scores within each category (within, beyond, and about the text). Reports from the *Data Management* CD-ROM can be helpful in identifying and analyzing patterns.

Step 3. Look for patterns across the entire group. Even though students are reading at different levels, there may be some similar needs in terms of comprehending and processing.

Step 4. Go to the Interactive Read-Aloud continuum for the grade level.

Step 5. Look at the characteristics of texts and keep them in mind as you select books to read aloud to students.

Step 6. Select and sequence texts so that students will make connections between them and build on previous understandings.

Step 7. Look at the behaviors and understandings and think about your students' needs in terms of active thinking within, beyond, and about texts.

Step 8. Select goals to accomplish in your interactive read-aloud program.

Step 9. Plan an "opening" to each text that will help your students think more deeply about the text or notice important information and characteristics. The opening should be brief, just a few words to set readers up for successful understanding (see Chapter 15, *Teaching for Comprehending and Fluency, K–8*).

Step 10. Plan intentional conversation and "turn and talk" routines (see Chapter 18, *Teaching for Comprehending and Fluency, K–8*) to support your students' thinking as you think through the text together.

Step 11. Plan for writing about reading (optional element). Here, think about the specific demands of the texts on the Interactive Read-Aloud continuum. Then, look at the Writing About Reading continuum for the grade level. Look at the genres that are appropriate and the thinking that students are expected to do.

Step 12. Keep a class record of books read aloud so that you and the students can easily remember connections and make new ones.

Linking Assessment Information to Whole-Group Minilessons in a Reading Workshop

Step 1. Assess the class and find Benchmark Independent, Benchmark Instructional, and Recommended Placement levels.

Step 2. Look at the total scores on comprehension and scores within each category (within, beyond, and about the text).

Step 3. Look at the evidence of processing—strategic actions and analysis of sources of information (MSV).

Step 4. Look for patterns across the entire group. Even though students are reading at different levels, there may be some similar needs in terms of comprehending and processing.

Step 5. Go to the Interactive Read-Aloud continuum. Look at the behaviors and understandings to notice, teach, and support.

Step 6. Think about your students' needs in terms of active thinking within, beyond, and about texts.

Step 7. Select goals that lend themselves to effective teaching in minilessons.

Step 8. Plan a minilesson (or short series of lessons) to address the goals.

Step 9. Plan for writing about reading (optional element). Here, think about the specific demands of the texts on the Interactive Read-Aloud continuum. Then, look at the Writing About Reading continuum for the grade level. Look at the genres that are appropriate and the thinking that students are expected to do.

Step 10. Students write about reading during their independent work time, writing about books they have selected for independent reading.

Step 11. Use the list of behaviors and understandings to guide them in their writing.

Step 12. You may be using a reader's notebook for various forms of writing including dialogue letters. Prompt and look for evidence of behaviors and understandings in students' writing. (See *Teaching for Comprehending and Fluency* [Heinemann, 2006] for specific lessons on using a reader's notebook.)

Connecting the Assessment to a Core or Basal Reading Program

The correlation between information gained from Benchmark Assessments and a leveled book reading program is clear. Identification of the Benchmark Independent and Instructional levels will allow you to guide the selection of independent reading books and choose books for instruction that are at the optimal level for supporting young readers. You can read detailed descriptions of the levels with sample texts in *Leveled Books K–8: Matching Texts to Readers for Effective Teaching* (Heinemann, 2006) and find over 20,000 leveled book titles in *The Fountas and Pinnell Leveled Book List, K–8* (Heinemann, 2006) and at www.fountasandpinnellleveledbooks.com.

Benchmark Assessment results can inform more than leveled reading programs. You may be using for reading instruction a set of materials that is usually referred to as a "basal" or "core" system. Most systems consist of anthologies of written material. The anthology may include stories written especially for reading instruction or drawn from various works of literature. Selections are sequenced in the anthologies.

With a core or basal system, you still need to think about readability. Understanding the demands of the texts will help you support and teach your students more effectively. Many core programs involve students in small-group reading instruction in addition to whole-group reading in the core anthology. The whole-group reading is usually in the form of read-aloud or shared reading. The basal system ideally includes sets of leveled books to differentiate instruction. Figure 46 will help you make the connection between the Fountas & Pinnell Benchmark Assessment System Instructional level and the basal system if you are using the anthology stories for small-group teaching. Use the benchmark books and their characteristics to help you "level" the materials in your basal system.

Level Correspondence—Core or Basal Reading Programs

Fountas and Pinnell Benchmark Instructional Level	Guided Reading Level (for instruction)	Basal System Level
A	A	Kindergarten
B	B	Kindergarten
C	C	Preprimer
D	D	Preprimer
E	E	Preprimer
F	F	Primer
G	G	Primer
H	H	Grade 1 (middle)
I	I	Grade 1 (late)
J	J	Grade 2 (early)
K	K	Grade 2 (early)
L	L	Grade 2 (late)
M	M	Grade 2 (late)
N	N	Grade 3 (early)
O	O	Grade 3 (early)
P	P	Grade 3 (late)
Q	Q	Grade 4 (early)
R	R	Grade 4 (early)
S	S	Grade 4 (late)
T	T	Grade 5 (early)
U	U	Grade 5 (early)
V	V	Grade 5 (late)
W	W	Grade 6 (early)
X	X	Grade 6 (early)
Y	Y	Grade 6 (late)
Z	Z	Grades 7 and 8

Figure 46. Benchmark levels correlated to guided reading and core textbook levels

Case Studies: Interpreting and Using Benchmark Assessment Data

The interpretation and use of Benchmark Assessment data are more important than the scores themselves. In this section, we present four examples of readers, along with our interpretations and teacher commentary.

Francesco, Grade 3 Student

In Figures 47–49, you see pages of Francesco's Recording Form, with fluency ratings, for levels M, N, and O; his Assessment Summary (Figure 50); and his Vocabulary in Context assessment for Level N (Figure 51).

Based on looking at Francesco's records from the previous year, the teacher, Mrs. Wahlberg, predicted that he would be reading slightly below grade level. She started the assessment on level L but found that the nonfiction text was easy for Francesco, although he read somewhat slowly. On level M, Francesco read the fiction text *Saving Up* (See Figure 47) with 98% accuracy and satisfactory comprehension, although, again, he read slowly. He self-corrected three times and appealed once, but after making an attempt. He demonstrated the ability to take multisyllabic words apart (for example, *responsible*), but gave up on the high frequency word *enough*. Overall, this text on level M seemed easy for Francesco.

On level N, Francesco read the nonfiction text *Dogs at Work* with 95% accuracy and satisfactory comprehension. This text was within instructional range, but it was also evident that Francesco was making careless errors, such as *the* for *their*, sometimes not attending to whether the error made sense or sounded like correct language structure (for example, "Guard dogs help blind people . . ." for "Guide dogs help blind people . . ."). He had four self-corrections, indicating the ability to monitor his reading. On this reading, his hesitance at multisyllable words was also evident.

continued on page 76

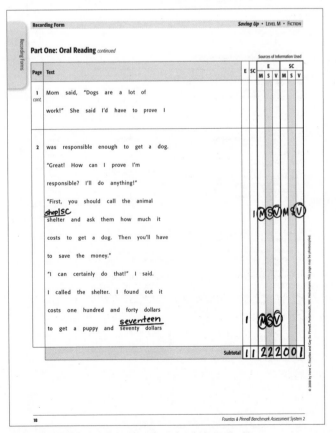

Figure 47a. Francesco's Recording form, level M, *Saving Up*

Figure 47b. Francesco's Recording form, level M, *Saving Up*

Level M—Benchmark Independent

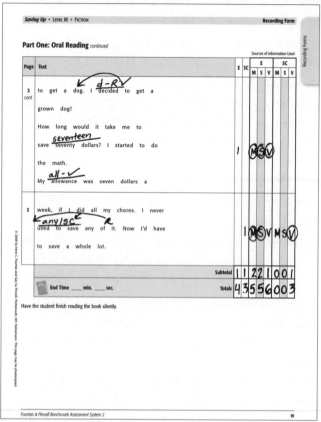

Figure 47c. Francesco's Recording form, level M, *Saving Up*

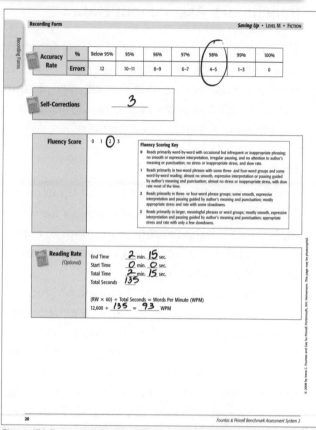

Figure 47d. Francesco's Recording form, level M, *Saving Up*

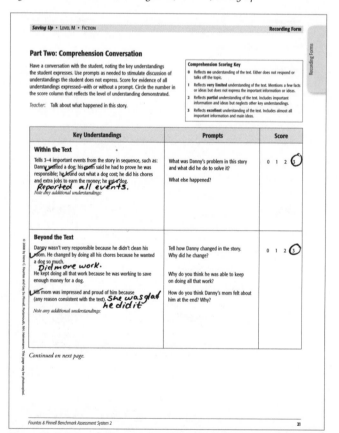

Figure 47e. Francesco's Recording form, level M, *Saving Up*

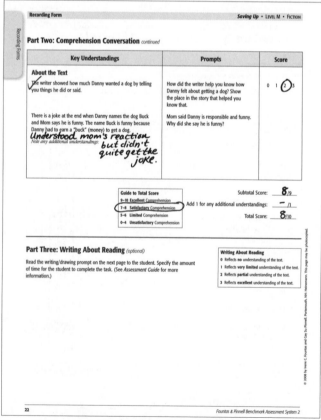

Figure 47f. Francesco's Recording form, level M, *Saving Up*

Level N—Benchmark Instructional

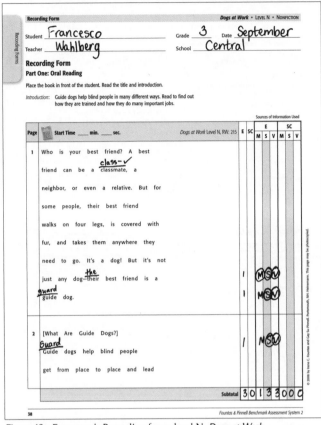

Figure 48a. Francesco's Recording form, level N, *Dogs at Work*

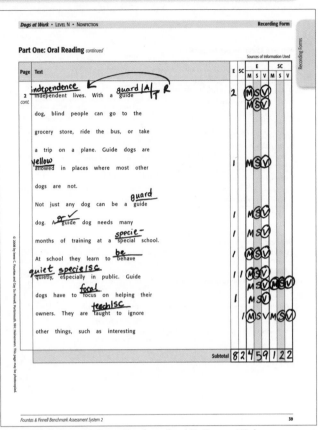

Figure 48b. Francesco's Recording form, level N, *Dogs at Work*

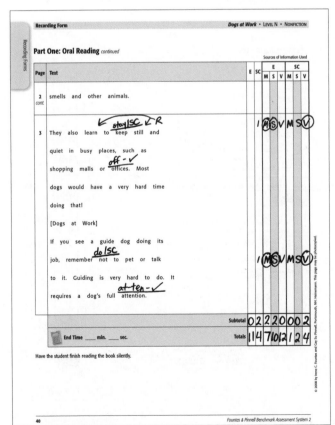

Figure 48c. Francesco's Recording form, level N, *Dogs at Work*

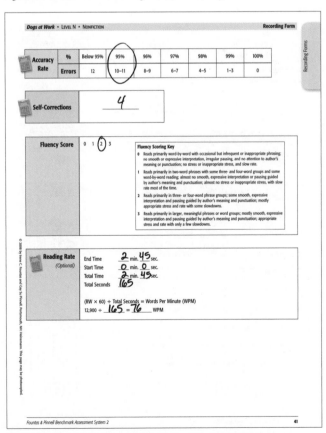

Figure 48d. Francesco's Recording form, level N, *Dogs at Work*

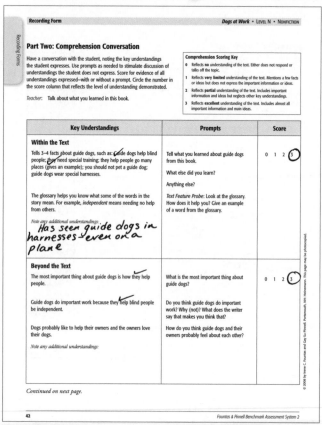

Figure 48e. Francesco's Recording form, level N, *Dogs at Work*

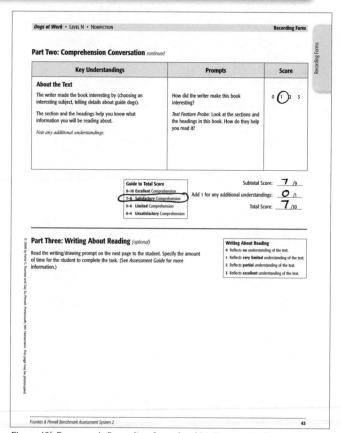

Figure 48f. Francesco's Recording form, level N, *Dogs at Work*

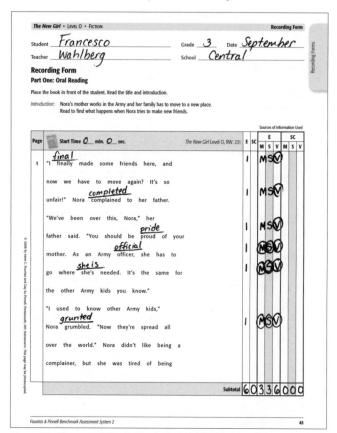

Figure 49a. Francesco's Recording form, level O, *The New Girl*

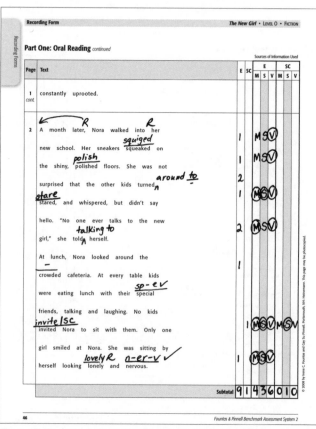

Figure 49b. Francesco's Recording form, level O, *The New Girl*

Level O—Hard Text

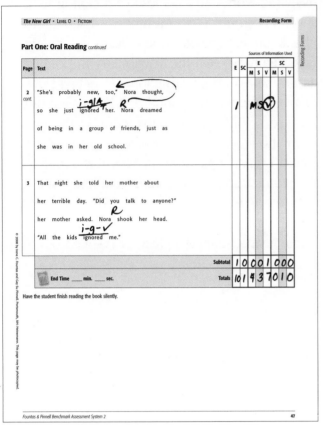

Figure 49c. Francesco's Recording form, level O, *The New Girl*

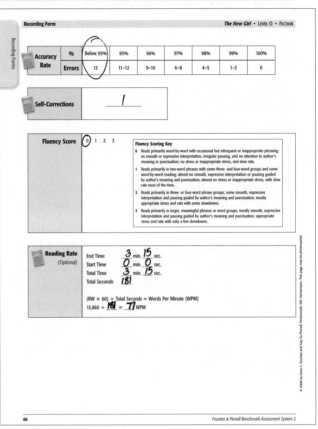

Figure 49d. Francesco's Recording form, level O, *The New Girl*

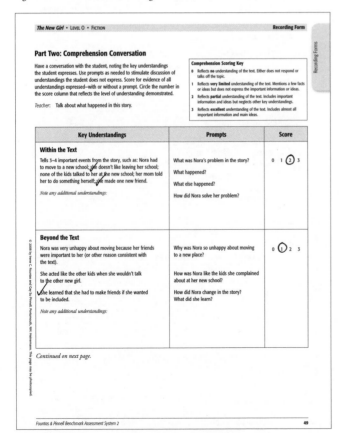

Figure 49e. Francesco's Recording form, level O, *The New Girl*

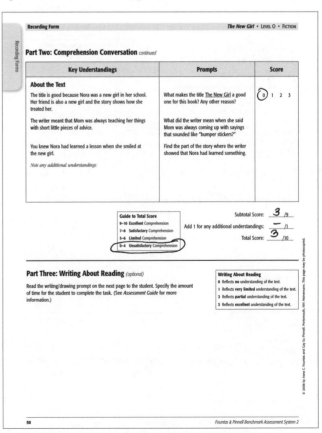

Figure 49f. Francesco's Recording form, level O, *The New Girl*

Mrs. Wahlberg had Francesco read the fiction text at level O, *The New Girl*, but his accuracy level was below 95% and his comprehension was unsatisfactory. Thinking that Francesco might not have been interested in the theme or character, the teacher tried the nonfiction level as well. The level O nonfiction text, *Snake Myths*, was hard for Francesco. He read the text at below 95% accuracy and his comprehension was unsatisfactory.

As evidenced by the kinds of errors he made on all his reading, Francesco was not attending closely to visual information or to language structure. His errors were evidence that he was not attending closely to print information. His processing almost broke down on harder text. While his reading was fast, there was little evidence of phrasing or intonation. Francesco appeared to be processing the text in a very mechanical way.

Because of Francesco's hesitance at multisyllable words and his loss of meaning with several errors, Mrs. Wahlberg decided to check on Francesco's vocabulary in context (see Figure 51). On the Vocabulary in Context assessment for the instructional-level text *Dogs at Work*, the teacher found that Francesco did have some difficulty with the words in this text even though he had satisfactory comprehension overall. For example, he was able to define the words *relative* and *handler*, but had trouble with the word *guide* as used in this text. Mrs. Wahlberg decided that level N was the appropriate instructional-level text for Francesco.

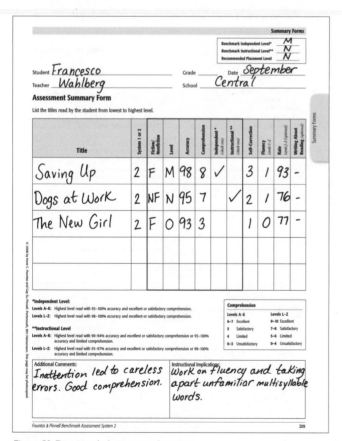

Figure 50. Francesco's Assessment Summary

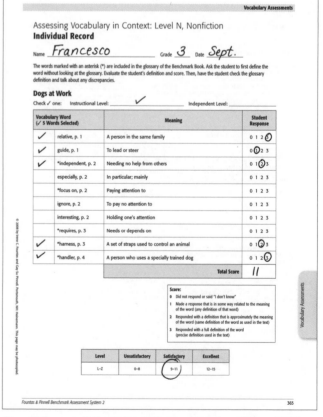

Figure 51. Francesco's Vocabulary in Context Assessment (*Dogs at Work*)

Mrs. Wahlberg Talks About Francesco

Analysis of Assessment. I was pleased to see that Francesco is doing grade-level reading. He did very well on levels L and M, so I think that he will be able to benefit from independent reading around those levels.

He knows a large number of high frequency words and these help him concentrate on meaning while reading easier texts. When he read the level N text, Francesco had more difficulty with multisyllable words. Sometimes he made almost no attempt to solve an unknown word. He would say the first part of the word and seemed to just think of anything to finish it. I also noticed that he made a lot of careless errors—either not thinking about how his reading sounded or not using enough of the visual information. On the difficult text at level O, his processing broke down. He did not get the overall point of the book *Snake Myths*. For example, he just reported that snakes have eyes and skin. Even when I questioned him about the myths, he could only say that they were stories about snakes, with no comment on how the facts show that the stories are mistaken beliefs.

Overall, I'd like for him to work more actively at making a text make sense and sound right, and I would also like more careful attention to the visual features of words.

Also, his reading was not fluent. Even on easy texts, he tended to read slowly. Interestingly, he read faster on the most difficult text, but many times he was sliding over the words and just saying anything that would enable him to move on. He skipped an entire line without noticing.

The Continuum as a Resource. After seeing Francesco's reading of a difficult text, I think it is important for him to read texts that he can process. As I work with him on level N, I have the overall goal of helping him think more actively as he reads, particularly getting the big ideas and using background knowledge. I think he could benefit from noticing some of the characteristics of genre. He needs strategies for figuring out the meaning of words from context, and I also need to teach him how to take apart longer words.

Looking at *The Continuum of Literacy Learning*, I have selected these goals for my immediate lessons:

▶ Use the context of a sentence, paragraph, or whole text to determine the meaning of a word.

▶ Solve words of two or three syllables, words with inflectional endings, and complex letter-sound relationships.

▶ Make predictions based on personal experiences, content knowledge, and knowledge of similar texts.

▶ Search for information to confirm or disconfirm predictions.

Figure 52. Mrs. Wahlberg's comments on Francesco's reading and her plans for instruction

Continued on next page

- ▶ Before, during, and after reading, bring background knowledge to the understanding of a text.

- ▶ Synthesize information across a longer text.

- ▶ Infer the big ideas or themes of a text.

- ▶ Notice and discuss aspects of genres—realistic and historical fiction, biography and other nonfiction, fantasy.

- ▶ Notice underlying organizational structures (description, compare-contrast, temporal sequence, problem/solution, cause-and-effect).

For word work, I plan to use white board demonstration to show him how to

- ▶ take apart longer words

- ▶ separate base words from endings

- ▶ figure out the meaning from context

Interactive read-aloud and literature discussion will also be helpful to Francesco in expanding his vocabulary and thinking about texts. He needs to engage in a great deal of talk that is grounded in texts.

Figure 52. Mrs. Wahlberg's comments on Francesco's reading and her plans for instruction, *continued*

Forest, Grade 5 Student

In Figures 53–56, you see pages of Forest's Recording Form, with fluency ratings, for levels T, U, and V (Figures 53, 54, and 55) and his Assessment Summary (Figure 56).

Forest read *Why Do Wolves Howl?*, a nonfiction level T, at 98% accuracy and excellent comprehension (see Figure 53). His reading was fluent during most of the oral reading. His substitution of *fierce* for *ferocious* made sense within the text, was the correct part of speech (fit the language structure), and also was related visually. During the comprehension conversation, he was able to discuss several important facts about wolves. More than factual material, he compared wolves to families and discussed how their howling helps them communicate many different meanings.

He read the nonfiction text *Earthquakes* (level U) at 96% accuracy, again making only a few errors, and reading fluently. When he encountered an unfamiliar word, he made a quick try at it and moved on. He finished the silent reading quickly as well and answered questions, indicating a satisfactory comprehension score.

Forest's next text was *A Call for a Change* (level V), which he read with 95% accuracy. He read more slowly this time but kept his momentum going. Forest had few self-corrections and moved on quickly after making attempts at unfamiliar words. He seemed to be using visual information consistently, but not looking at all parts of the words he did not know. Also, he did little repeating to be sure that what he was reading made sense. On the comprehension conversation for this book, Forest scored only 4. A major barrier to his understanding was the genre of the text. While the text is fiction, it takes the form of a persuasive essay (writing to persuade the mayor and city council to create a youth center, Rachel first identifies the problem and then proposes a solution). Forest did understand that there was a problem with teenagers hanging around with nothing to do. But he did not understand or remember Rachel's specific proposal. His comprehension score indicates that this level is too hard.

Because of Forest's difficulty with comprehension, Mr. Bradshaw decided that level U is an appropriate placement level for Forest (see Figure 57); however, he will work intensively on comprehension and continue to support Forest's excellent word-solving strategies. Forest should move quickly to the next level.

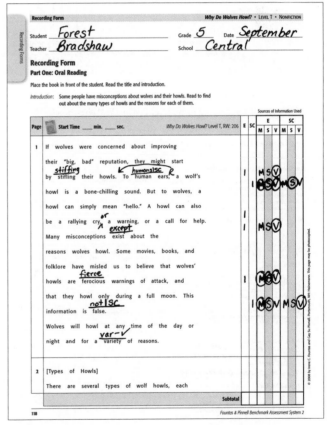

Figure 53a. Forest's Recording form, level T, *Why Do Wolves Howl?*

Level T—Benchmark Independent

Figure 53b. Forest's Recording form, level T, *Why Do Wolves Howl?*

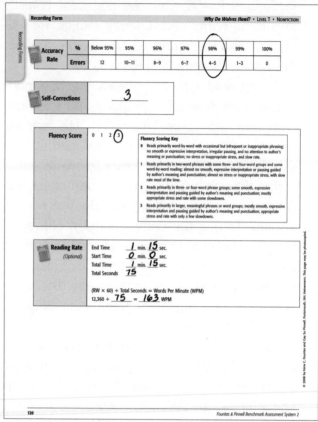

Figure 53c. Forest's Recording form, level T, *Why Do Wolves Howl?*

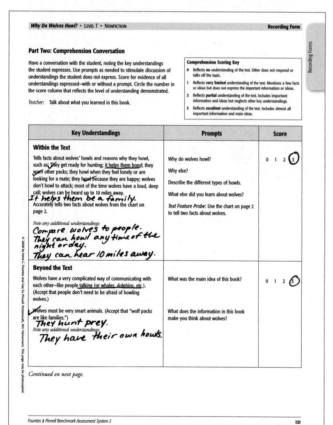

Figure 53d. Forest's Recording form, level T, *Why Do Wolves Howl?*

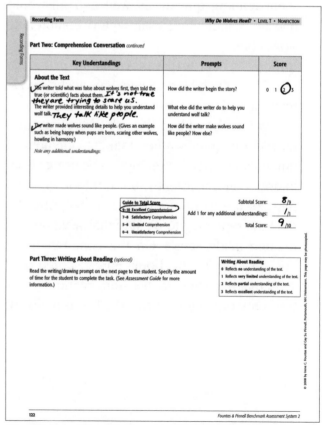

Figure 53e. Forest's Recording form, level T, *Why Do Wolves Howl?*

Level U—Benchmark Instructional

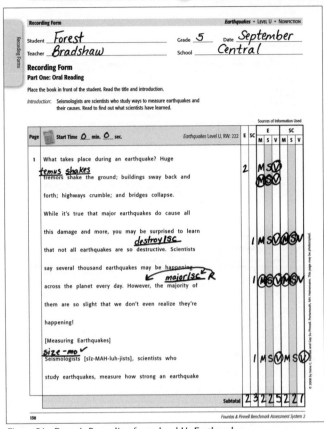

Figure 54a. Forest's Recording form, level U, *Earthquakes*

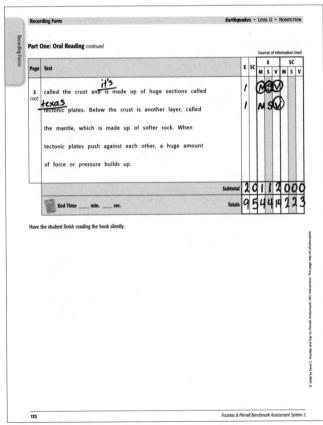

Figure 54c. Forest's Recording form, level U, *Earthquakes*

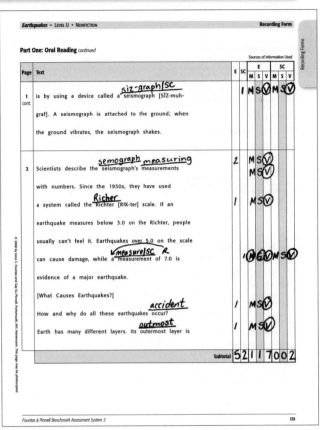

Figure 54b. Forest's Recording form, level U, *Earthquakes*

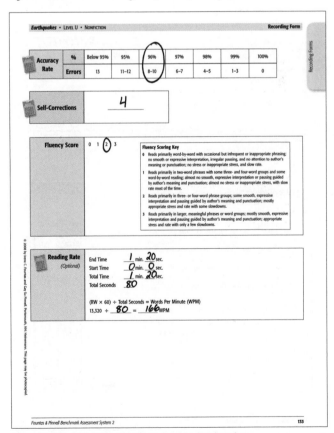

Figure 54d. Forest's Recording form, level U, *Earthquakes*

Level U (continued) and Level V

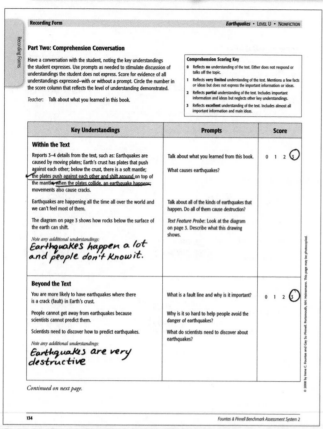

Figure 54e. Forest's Recording form, level U, *Earthquakes*

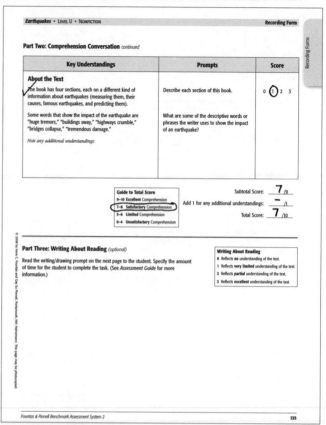

Figure 54f. Forest's Recording form, level U, *Earthquakes*

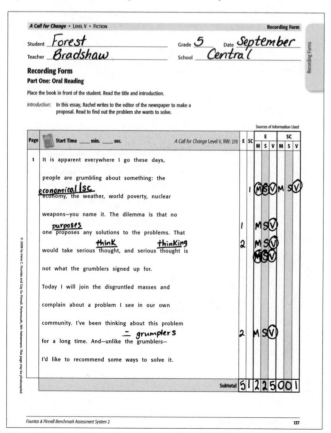

Figure 55a. Forest's Recording form, level V, *A Call for a Change*

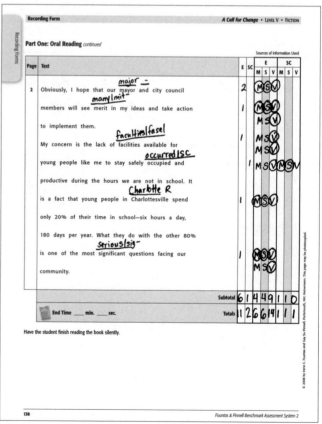

Figure 55b. Forest's Recording form, level V, *A Call for a Change*

Level V *(continued)*—Hard Text

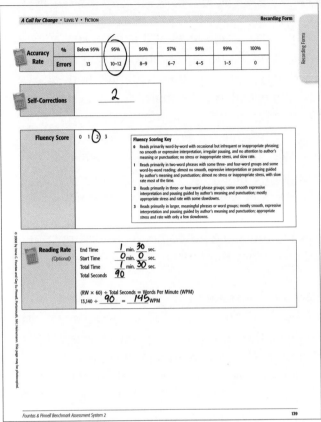

Figure 55c. Forest's Recording form, level V, *A Call for a Change*

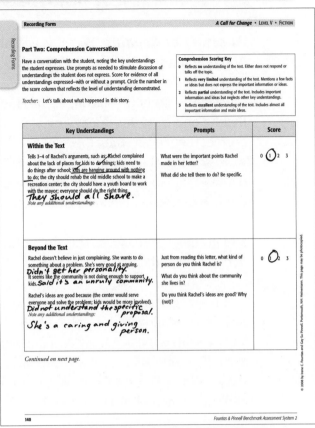

Figure 55d. Forest's Recording form, level V, *A Call for a Change*

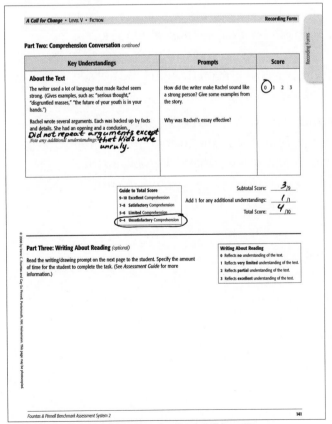

Figure 55e. Forest's Recording form, level V, *A Call for a Change*

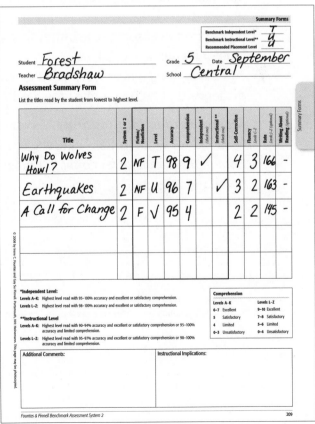

Figure 56. Forest's Assessment Summary

Mr. Bradshaw talks about Forest

Analysis of Reading. Forest is actually reading above grade level at this time. His oral reading sounds very fluent and expressive at level T, and his comprehension is excellent. On the next higher level, he also read very well, with 96% accuracy and satisfactory comprehension. Again, his fluency was excellent, although I did notice that he achieved this fluency by making quick attempts at words and not working to correct them even when they did not make sense in the sentence. Forest has excellent word-solving ability, but he may need to slow down and think more about whether his reading is accurate and sounds right. I thought he might have been thrown by the use of present tense. I notice that some of his errors were related to substituting words in past tense. Maybe it was especially difficult because the text had many long and complex sentences. This did not really seem to influence his comprehension or fluency, but it did lower his accuracy. Without those errors, this text would have been an easy one for him.

I really thought the level U text seemed easy for Forest, and I predicted that the next level would also be within instructional range. Again, he read *A Call for Change*, level V, with good accuracy and fluency, but I noticed the same pattern when it came to making one attempt at a word and not monitoring when the reading didn't make sense. When Forest talked with me about this text, it was evident that he had not really understood it. He remembered that there was a problem with kids hanging around the streets with nothing to do, but he did not show evidence of understanding that Rachel had described the problem and proposed a solution. I am even wondering whether Forest was concentrating during the silent part of the reading or even if he skipped over some of it. Either way, it is a problem because he may tend to skip or fade out when a text is harder.

I really think that Forest has good word-solving strategies even though I did not see evidence that he is working very hard at making his reading accurate.

Instructional Implications. I plan to engage Forest in instructional reading at level U and work to help him engage more deeply in the texts he reads. From the *Continuum of Literacy Learning*, I have selected these goals for small-group instructional reading:

Figure 57. Mr. Bradshaw's comments on Forest's reading and his plans for instruction

- ▶ Process long sentences (twenty or more words) with embedded clauses (prepositional phrases, introductory clauses, series of nouns, verbs, or adverbs).

- ▶ Use a wide range of word-solving strategies including dividing words into syllables and using prefixes and affixes.

- ▶ Express changes in ideas or perspective across the reading (as events unfold) and/or after reading a text.

- ▶ Notice and discuss aspects of genres—realistic and historical fiction; fantasy; myths and legends, biography, autobiography, memoir, and diaries; and other nonfiction "hybrid texts."

- ▶ Discuss the selection of genre in relation to inferred writer's purpose for a range of texts.

- ▶ Notice aspects of a writer's craft (style, language, perspective, themes) after reading several texts by the same author.

- ▶ Notice how authors use words in a connotative way to imply something beyond the literal meaning.

- ▶ Notice the use of figurative or descriptive language and talk about how it adds to the quality (enjoyment and understanding) of a text.

I do not think Forest needs a great deal of word work, but I do want to check to see whether he is noticing word parts such as affixes. If not, he will need to spend some time on this aspect of word study. I can help through minilessons or during guided reading. My greater priority is to help him think actively about his reading.

Figure 57. Mr. Bradshaw's comments on Forest's reading and his plans for instruction *(continued)*

Tanicia, Grade 7 Student

In Figures 58, 59, and 61 you see pages of Tanicia's Recording Form, with fluency ratings, for levels X, Y, and Z; her writing about reading response at level Y (Figure 60); and her Assessment Summary (Figure 62).

Before reading *A Weighty Decision*, Tanicia read texts at levels U, V, and W with ease and fluency. Her reading of *A Weighty Decision*, level X, was almost perfect in terms of accuracy and was also fluent. During the comprehension conversation, Tanicia talked enthusiastically about the issues in this text. She understood the idea of athletic competition and temptation to take diet pills. She missed only one word, *leviathan*, which did not undermine her comprehension. She also understood the descriptive language of the text. In effectively processing this text, she handled very long and complex sentences. Processing a text at this level means that Tanicia has developed a very effective processing system.

Tanicia read *The International Space Station*, level Y, again at high accuracy (96%). Most of her errors could be attributed to reading quickly and not noticing unimportant errors (*would* for *could*). In the comprehension conversation, she discussed the importance of the space station and some of the problems to be overcome before people can take long voyages in space—for example, finding ways to get water and food and ways to exercise. She did not pick up the idea that there might be psychological difficulties for people staying a long time in space, but she did have adequate comprehension, although her written response (see Figure 60) was at a fairly superficial level.

It was obvious that Tanicia was an excellent reader. On level Z, *Surviving the Blitz*, she read with 96% accuracy. Two of her errors were related to words from a language other than English. She was an excellent decoder of words. But during the comprehension conversation, she had difficulty with much of the meaning of the text. This text has a very heavy load of figurative language. For example, the writer uses the metaphor of a cat stalking mice over a fairly extensive portion of the text to symbolize the kind of fear that the British felt during the *blitzkrieg*. Her score on comprehension was 4, indicating that despite her decoding abilities, this text was difficult for her.

Figure 63 shows how Tanicia's teacher, Ms. Scott, thought through the assessment results and the instructional decisions based on them.

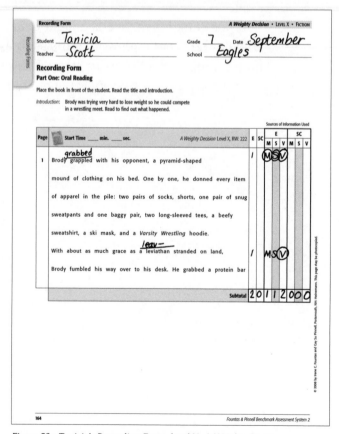

Figure 58a. Tanicia's Recording Form, level X, *A Weighty Decision*

Level X—Benchmark Independent

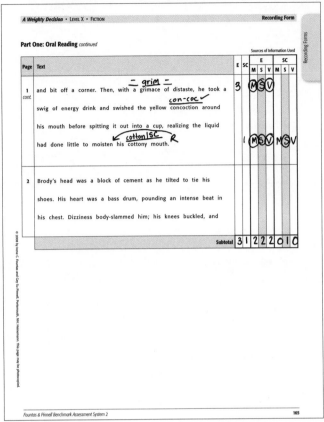

Figure 58b. Tanicia's Recording Form, level X, *A Weighty Decision*

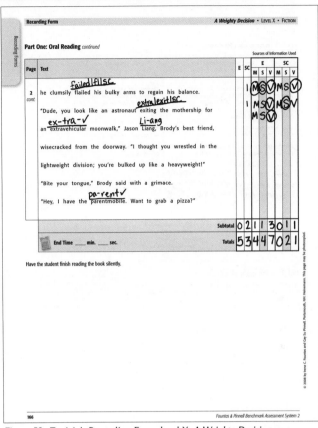

Figure 58c. Tanicia's Recording Form, level X, *A Weighty Decision*

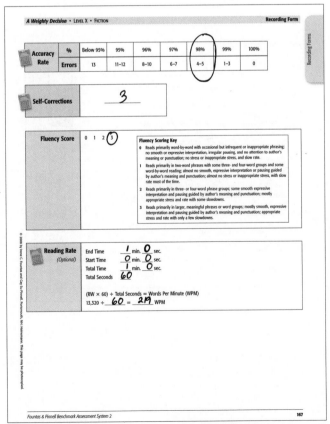

Figure 58d. Tanicia's Recording Form, level X, *A Weighty Decision*

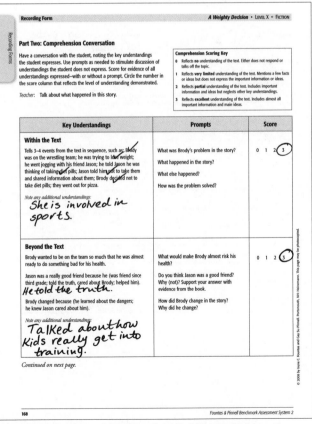

Figure 58e. Tanicia's Recording Form, level X, *A Weighty Decision*

Level X *(continued)* and Level Y—Benchmark Instructional

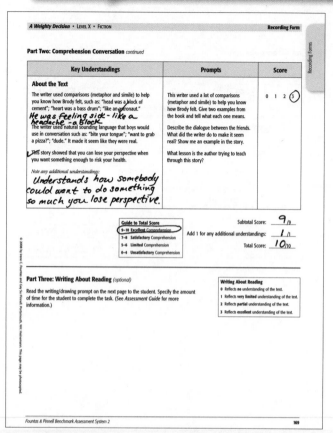

Figure 58f. Tanicia's Recording Form, level X, *A Weighty Decision*

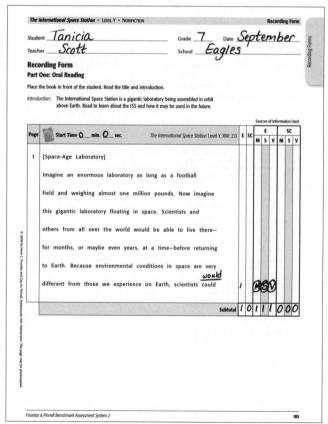

Figure 59a. Tanicia's Recording Form, level Y, *The International Space Station*

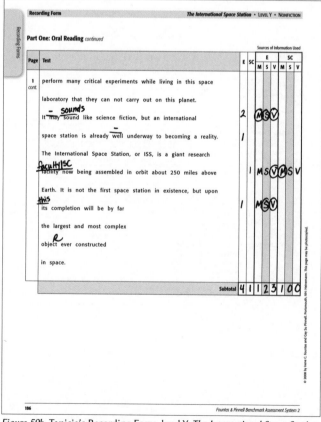

Figure 59b. Tanicia's Recording Form, level Y, *The International Space Station*

Level Y—Benchmark Instructional

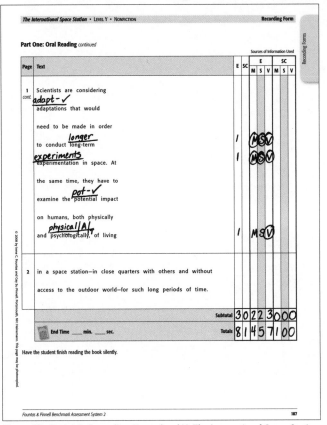

Figure 59c. Tanicia's Recording Form, level Y, *The International Space Station*

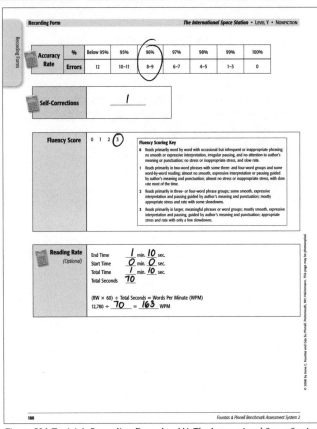

Figure 59d. Tanicia's Recording Form, level Y, *The International Space Station*

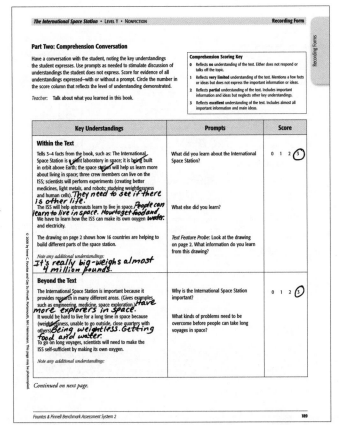

Figure 59e. Tanicia's Recording Form, level Y, *The International Space Station*

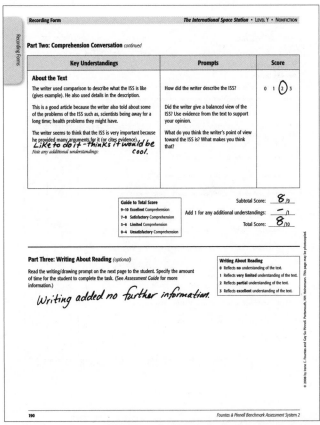

Figure 59f. Tanicia's Recording Form, level Y, *The International Space Station*

The International Space Station • LEVEL Y • NONFICTION — Recording Form

Student _____ Tanicia _____ Date _____

Write a short article explaining why the space station is important for the future. You can draw a sketch to go with your writing.

So that we would have more information about outer space and to see if their was other forms of life a to see how it would treat with the human body. So we could learn more about outer space.

Figure 60. Tanicia's writing, *The International Space Station*

Recording Form — **Surviving the Blitz** • LEVEL Z • FICTION

Student _Tanicia_   Grade _7_   Date _September_
Teacher _____   School _Eagles_

Recording Form
Part One: Oral Reading

Place the book in front of the student. Read the title and introduction.

Introduction: An 11-year-old, Margaret Davies, tells about her terrifying experience during World War II. Read to learn about her memories of the time.

Start Time 0 min. 0 sec.   *Surviving the Blitz* Level Z, RW: 215

Page	Text	Sources of Information Used

1. What was it like to experience London's infamous Blitz? I can tell you in one word: terrifying.
Blitz is short for blitzkrieg—the German words for lightning (*blitz*) and war (*krieg*). The Blitz was our British newspapers' term for the German bombing that barraged London in 1940 and 1941 during World War II, a war that had begun about a year earlier when France and Britain declared war on Germany. Although World War II ended over sixty years ago, still the bombs of the Blitz scream toward me and explode into terrifying nightmares.

Subtotal 3 1 1 1 2 0 0 1

Figure 61a. Tanicia's Recording Form, level Z, *Surviving the Blitz*

Surviving the Blitz • LEVEL Z • FICTION — Recording Form

Part One: Oral Reading *continued*

Page	Text	E	SC	E (M S V)	SC (M S V)

1 *cont.* I, Margaret Davies, was only 11 years of age when the bombs began raining down. (Unfortunately, *blitzkrieg* was an apt expression!) Bombs fell from the sky for 57 days in a row, shattering our lives, pulverizing our homes, and injuring or killing thousands. Whenever the air raid sirens wailed, my family rushed *en masse* out to the bomb shelter in the backyard—that terrible dark hole in the ground, tiny, cold, and damp— and sitting there trembling in the cacophony, as the bombs shrieked in and exploded, I felt as though the sky

2 itself were cracking open. The dank shelter flooded each time it rained, forcing us to hide instead under the stairs in our house, like mice in the wainscoting.

Subtotal 5 1 1 2 5 0 0 1
End Time ___ min. ___ sec.   Totals 8 2 2 3 7 0 0 2

Have the student finish reading the book silently.

Figure 61b. Tanicia's Recording Form, level Z, *Surviving the Blitz*

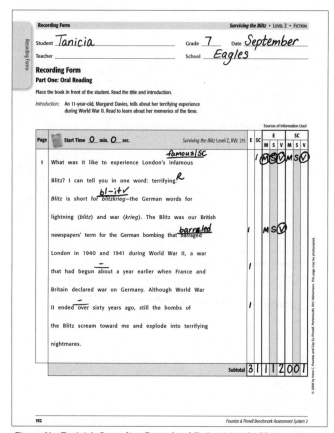

Level Z (continued)

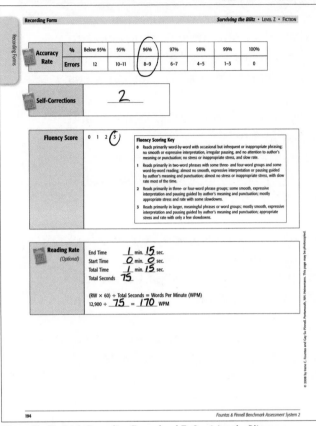

Figure 61c. Tanicia's Recording Form, level Z, *Surviving the Blitz*

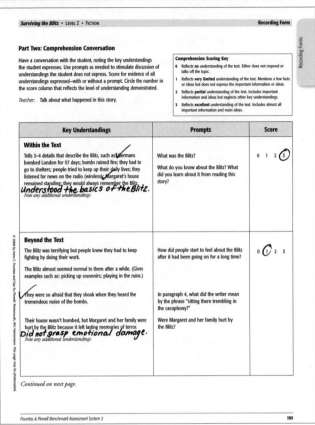

Figure 61d. Tanicia's Recording Form, level Z, *Surviving the Blitz*

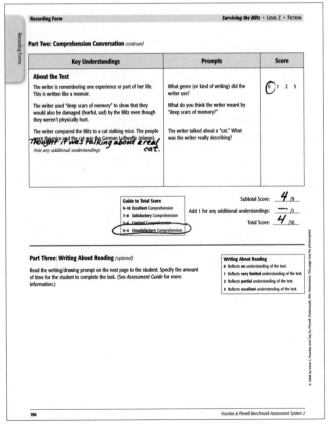

Figure 61e. Tanicia's Recording Form, level Z, *Surviving the Blitz*

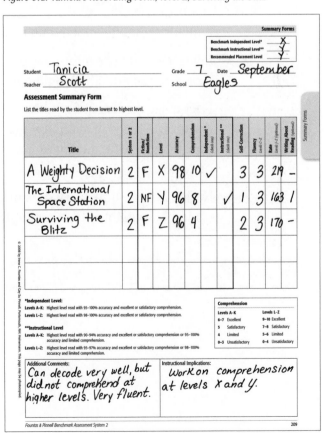

Figure 62. Tanicia's Assessment Summary

Ms. Scott Talks About Tanicia

Tanicia is an excellent reader. She has very good word-solving strategies and can read almost any text accurately. With this reader, I am not really worried about the level of text that she can read. She is almost at an adult level of reading except that she needs more experience with highly literary texts.

She really liked *A Weighty Decision*, maybe because she is involved in sports and connected with the text. This level of text was easy for her.

When she read *The International Space Station*, she also had very good accuracy and fluency. I thought her understanding was adequate but a little superficial. I could not get her to elaborate on what she thought about the space station.

When she read *Surviving the Blitz* at level Z, she again read with high accuracy. I am convinced that Tanicia can decode her way through just about any text. So I need to think how I can help her as a reader. During our conversation about the text, I noticed that she did not understand the central metaphor of the first part of the text. I think Tanicia got the general idea of the *blitz* but she did not understand some of the subtleties of the text.

I will probably be involving Tanicia in literature discussion groups and individual conferences. I may include her in some small-group teaching sessions at level Y, although books for this group could be at a variety of levels—W, X, Y, or Z. As I look at the *Continuum of Literacy Learning*, I can identify some goals as:

- ▶ Use a full range of readers' tools to search for information (table of contents, glossary, headings/subheadings, callouts, pronunciation guides, index, references).

- ▶ Search for and use information in a wide range of graphics (some dense and challenging, requiring information).

- ▶ Recognize the use of figurative or descriptive language (or special types of language such as irony) and talk about how it adds to the quality (enjoyment and understanding) of a text.

- ▶ Notice how authors use words in a connotative way (to imply something beyond the literal meaning).

Figure 63. Ms. Scott's comments on Tanicia's reading and plans for instruction

Using the Benchmark Assessment System with English Language Learners

One question that always arises when implementing an assessment system is: How does a student's understanding of English affect the results? When working with English language learners, we must consistently work to understand all the texts they read from their unique point of view. For example, the speaker's understanding of the syntax of her own language may be strong, but English syntax poses a challenge. Thus, that source of information is not strong. Also, students may learn to decode English but not understand the meaning of words because they have a more limited oral vocabulary than native English speakers. Let's look at two reading records for English language learners.

Peti, Grade 2 English Language Learner

Peti entered the third grade in January after coming to the U.S. from Cambodia and began to learn English at that time. She is now in fourth grade. In Figure 64 on the next page, you see the record of her reading of *Vanessa's Butterfly* (Level N).

Peti read *Vanessa's Butterfly* at below 95% accuracy. Her substitutions indicated strong awareness of visual features of words. For example, she substituted *read* (long *e*) for *read* (short *e* sound), *mother* for *mother's, land* for *landed*, and *flows* for *flowers*. It may be that Peti was not noticing the ends of words but it is more likely that she was not monitoring using the syntax of English. Her substitutions may reflect her oral English at this time. She was using meaning, as indicated by her self-correction of the substitution *working* for *watering*; however, the errors throughout, without self-correction, resulted in limited comprehension. She was able to state that the name *Vanessa* means *butterfly*, that she wanted to catch it, and that she decided it should be free. She also inferred that Vanessa felt that the butterfly should be free because her name meant butterfly. She also described the wing zigzags as an example of how the writer described the butterfly. But the score on comprehension was 6, which is at the limited level. Level N is too difficult for Peti at this time, but she is showing many strengths as a reader. She can read many high frequency words and shows good word-solving ability. Even though she has some difficulty with syntax, she is approaching satisfactory comprehension of the text. As additional information, she read quickly, but she gave little attention to punctuation and there was little intonation. It may be that Peti is concentrating on word solving at the expense of meaning and fluency. Her instructional level will be lower than N, probably M or possibly L. The important thing is to find a text that she can read with sufficient accuracy and comprehension to make instruction effective. At a slightly lower level, Peti will be able to use her strengths to work on what sounds right (with English syntax) in connection with looking at the ends of words. In addition, she will be able to enter into discussions of texts to gain a deeper meaning. She would benefit from participation in reader's theater to gain familiarity with syntax.

Level N—Benchmark Instructional

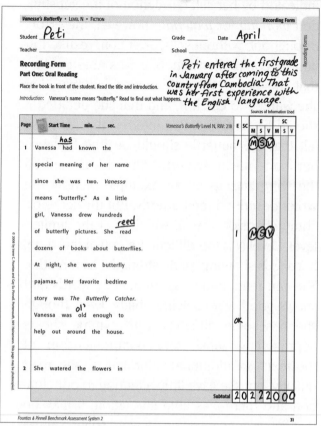

Figure 64a. Peti's Recording Form, level N, *Vanessa's Butterfly*

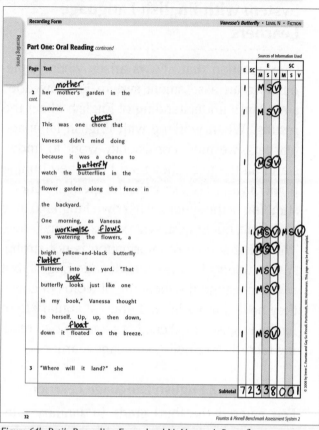

Figure 64b. Peti's Recording Form, level N, *Vanessa's Butterfly*

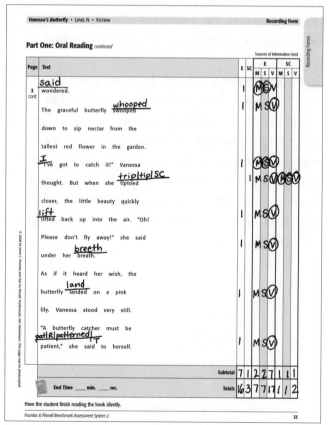

Figure 64c. Peti's Recording Form, level N, *Vanessa's Butterfly*

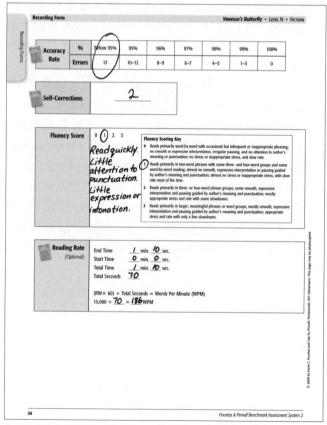

Figure 64d. Peti's Recording Form, level N, *Vanessa's Butterfly*

Level N—Benchmark Instructional *(continued)*

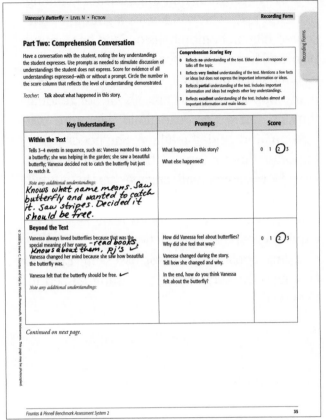

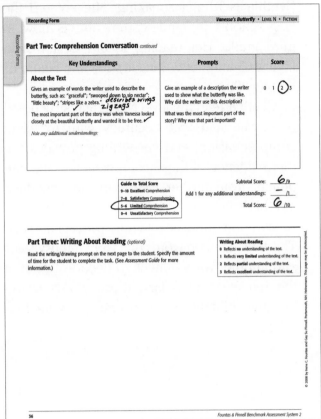

Figure 64e. Peti's Recording Form, level N, *Vanessa's Butterfly*

Figure 64f. Peti's Recording Form, level N, *Vanessa's Butterfly*

Cynthia, Grade 3 English Language Learner

Cynthia is Khmer speaking. She entered the U.S. schools in kindergarten and is now in third grade. Her reading record is shown in Figure 65 and her writing is shown in Figure 67 on page 99.

Cynthia read the level N text at instructional level. She had 95% accuracy with excellent comprehension, and her writing provides further evidence of these competencies. She can benefit from further instruction in decoding, but this is not her most important problem. Her substitutions indicate difficulty with vocabulary. This text included words that were multisyllabic and in other ways difficult to decode. If not in the reader's vocabulary, these words would be quite difficult, even to attempt. With hav-

ing "tolds" from the teacher, Cynthia was able to access the words and to construct meaning from the text, which indicates a strength. She scored high in comprehension, and her writing provided further evidence of her understanding. Cynthia's instructional level is N, but she needs many opportunities to talk about her reading through interactive read-aloud, literature discussion, and guided reading. She needs many opportunities to expand her English vocabulary. Her teacher will engage her in guided reading at Level N and will be sure that there is a rich conversation around texts as well as explicit vocabulary instruction.

Some considerations for assessing English language learners' reading are summarized in Figure 66.

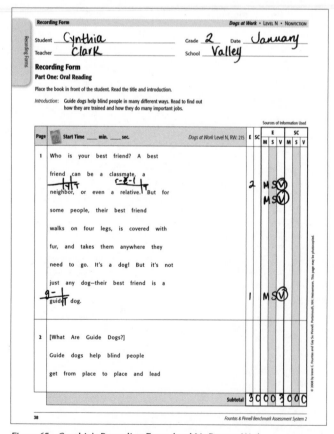

Figure 65a. Cynthia's Recording Form, level N, *Dogs at Work*

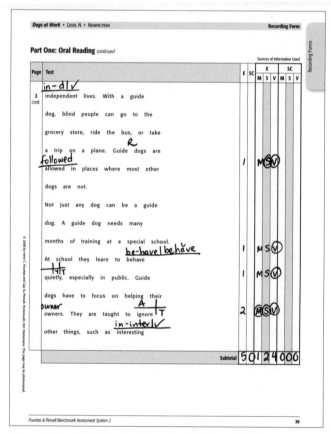

Figure 65b. Cynthia's Recording Form, level N, *Dogs at Work*

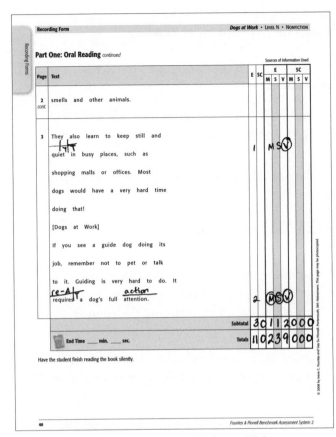

Figure 65c. Cynthia's Recording Form, level N, *Dogs at Work*

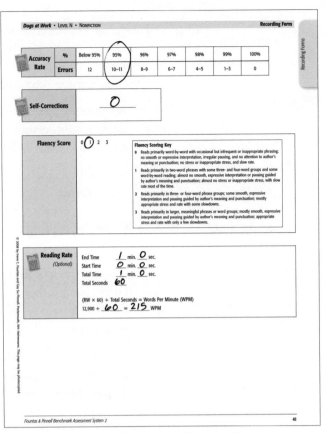

Figure 65d. Cynthia's Recording Form, level N, *Dogs at Work*

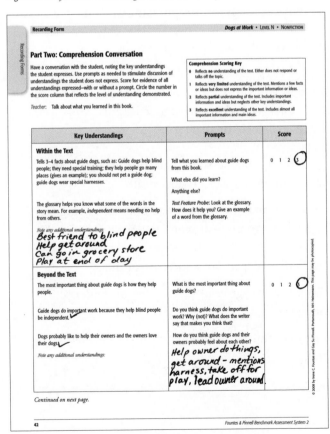

Figure 65e. Cynthia's Recording Form, level N, *Dogs at Work*

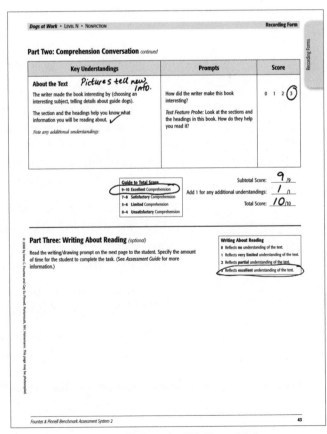

Figure 65f. Cynthia's Recording Form, level N, *Dogs at Work*

English Language Learners: Considerations for Assessment of Reading	
Administration	▶ Follow your district policy regarding the level of English proficiency required for standardized assessment. ▶ Administer the assessment with the standardized procedures. If a student does not understand directions or a question, paraphrase so the student will know what is required. ▶ Discontinue the student's reading of a benchmark book when it is clearly too difficult.
Coding and scoring	▶ Code the reading using the standard conventions. ▶ If the errors that a student makes appear to be related to the influence of the student's first language, make a quick note on the Recording Form. For example, the student might apply the rules of syntax from the first language or have a particular way of enunciating the sounds in a word. ▶ In general, errors related to syntax are counted as errors. Use judgment in counting slight variations in pronunciation as errors, as they might be dialect differences. ▶ In addition to coding behaviors, you can make some quick notes on the form to help you remember any difficulties you think are due to the student's first language. Also make some notes on phrasing and fluency.
Analysis	▶ Analyze the student's use of sources of information using the standardized procedures. ▶ Make notes on your record when you think an error is related to a difference in the student's background knowledge, cultural knowledge, control of language structure, or dialect.
Fluency	▶ Take into account the fact that there may be some variation in stress and intonation based on the way a student speaks English orally. ▶ Take into account that some pauses may be related not only to solving the word but also to recalling what the English word means.
Comprehension	▶ Consider the content of a particular text in your interpretation. ▶ Realize that a student may lack the background knowledge or evidence a difference in cultural knowledge. ▶ Realize that some discrepancy may not be reading comprehension as much as it is language proficiency.

Figure 66. Considerations for reading assessment with English language learners

Continued on next page

English Language Learners: Considerations for Assessment of Reading *continued*	
Interpretation of the assessment	▷ Oral language is an important factor in the reading process. If a student has never heard a word, it will be more difficult for her to read it. She will likely rely more on using the visual information only.
	▷ If a student does not use a particular language structure, it will be difficult for her to use the structure of the language to anticipate new words.
	▷ If the context of the text is not meaningful to the student, it will be more difficult for him to use meaning as a guide to problem solve the words in the text.
	▷ Avoid placing the student in texts that are too difficult. You do not want the English language learner to rely only on calling words with little attention to meaning.

Figure 66. Considerations for reading assessment with English language learners (*continued*)

Figure 67. Cynthia's writing about reading, level N, *Dogs at Work*

Documenting Student Growth in Reading over Time

An assessment conference with the Fountas & Pinnell Benchmark Assessment System represents a student's reading at one point in time. Using standardized procedures and multiple leveled texts, the conference provides a reliable picture of the student's reading strengths and weaknesses at that time. Benchmark assessments that are taken two or three times during a year provide a good picture of a student's progress in the instructional program. Nevertheless, benchmark assessment results must always be understood within the perspective of the ongoing observation you do every day during reading instruction, especially at early levels. By using the benchmark assessment as a baseline, conducting informal observations, and coding oral reading on reading records at specific intervals, you can track the growth of individuals over time and gain valuable instructional information. You can also identify students who are going off track and provide planned intervention.

In this section, we examine ways of looking at individual progress over time and monitoring adequate progress.

Looking at Individual Progress

The Assessment Summary forms in the *Assessment Forms* book and CD-ROM provide a place to record a student's Benchmark Independent and Benchmark Instructional levels. There are versions for recording scores two (Bi-annual Assessment Summary), three (Tri-annual Assessment Summary), or four (Quarterly Assessment Summary) times a year. (The *Data Management* CD-ROM will update this report from the data entered at individual conferences.) These scores plot a student's progress over time and provide a clear picture of how the educational system is bringing the student forward as a reader.

In addition, two reading graphs can chart an individual's reading progress. The Annual Record of Reading Progress provides opportunities for noting the levels from Benchmark Assessment conferences and interim running records. The date and title of the book with the accuracy rate of the reading are entered onto the form and a symbol is placed on a grid; a line connecting the symbols provides a graph of progress. The Longitudinal Record of Reading Progress—found in the *Assessment Forms* book and CD-ROM as well as printed on the Student Folder—plots a student's Benchmark level (either Independent or Instructional) four times a year across all eight grades. The *Data Management* CD-ROM creates these graphs for you once you have entered the data.

Monitoring Adequate Progress

With typical progress, we would expect third graders at the beginning of the year to independently read texts at levels J, K, and L. They may select books at lower levels with content that is interesting to them. At the same time, they would be participating in small-group reading instruction using books around level M and N. By the end of the year, they will be reading these levels independently and reaching levels O or P with teacher support. Fourth graders at the beginning of the year will be independently reading levels N and O and participating in instruction at about levels P and Q, progressing by the end of the year to level S or T. Grade 5 students typically move from about levels S–W across a year, and grade 6 students from levels V–Y or Z.

In grades 7 and 8, students are typically able to read widely across levels W, X, Y, and Z. At levels V–Z, text difficulty is related to very complex interrelated factors. There may be high-level, technical vocabulary words and/or the sentences may be long and very complex. On the other hand, the words and sentences may be relatively easy, but the characters are complex or the story is hard to follow. Many texts at these levels assume that the reader has prior knowledge of the topic or understands significant aspects of the setting. At the highest levels, readers need deep understanding of genres and their characteristics; based on that knowledge, readers form expectations that support them in comprehending the text. And, the issues texts explore are often mature, requiring background knowledge and experience to understand. Except for the age-appropriate content, texts at level Y or Z are equivalent to or even more difficult than typical adult reading. Students who can read at these levels can probably also read adult material although often with limited understanding.

What all of this means is that effective reading at the highest levels is much more than decoding the words. Sometimes you will find that students can read high levels accurately at 98% and above; but their understanding of the ideas and content is only superficial. For a level to be appropriate, the reader must be able to think deeply and to articulate understandings in oral language or writing.

Benchmark Assessment will help you identify a student's Benchmark Instructional level and provides information that will help you recommend a placement level for instruction. The instructional level is important to know. Reading texts that demand a little more than a student's independent level—and instructional support—makes it possible to expand the reading processing system. Usually, this Benchmark Instructional level is also the Recommended Placement level, although as you look at the data, you may choose a lower or higher level for good reason.

The Benchmark Independent reading level is also important to know. It is on independent-level texts that students can read with high accuracy that they have the opportunity to smoothly orchestrate systems of strategic actions. Students who have formed the habit of reading dysfluently need to engage in a great deal of easy reading. Through independently reading books of their choice, they can:

- ▶ increase vocabulary

- ▶ build content knowledge that will be helpful in reading informational texts

- ▶ increase fluency

- ▶ build up their knowledge of how texts are organized

- ▶ learn how to select appropriate texts for themselves

Students choose their independent reading books according to interest rather than by level; but if they have learned how to select books appropriately, they can explore topics across a range of levels that they can read independently.

Your daily observations of reading behavior and systematic administration of the Benchmark Assessment System will help you notice and document progress so that you can determine when students need intervention. Students who are reading just below grade level need daily small-group instruction using a gradient of text. It will also be helpful to them to do a great deal of easy reading, supported by individual conferences in which you can support depth of thinking and coach for fluency. Those students who are reading a year or more below grade level will need intervention in the form of tutoring or small groups in addition to intensive classroom instruction. Some characteristics of effective interventions are:

- ▶ daily reading of continuous text at instructional level

- ▶ reading and rereading easier texts at independent level

- ▶ phonics and word work appropriate to the level

- ▶ writing in connection with reading

- ▶ intensive teaching by an individual with specialized skills

We do not recommend that students who are having difficulty be turned over to paraprofessionals or volunteers. These students need the most skilled teaching of all.

Case Study: Looking at a Reader Over Time

As one example of change over time in a school year, let's look at Henry's reading at five points in time, with assessment taking place twice a year, on pages 106–113. First, take a look at the Assessment Summary recorded in September of grade 3 (Figure 68). You'll notice that Henry read *City Hawks* (level M) at an independent level and had high comprehension. He was generally fluent, with a rating of 2. He then read *Vanessa's Butterfly* (level N) at 95% accuracy, with satisfactory comprehension and good fluency, which indicated that this would be a good instructional level for him (see Figure 69).

Overall, Henry's reading of the level N text indicated that he was monitoring his reading, self-correcting some errors, and using all sources of information. He made a few careless errors that he appeared not to notice (for example, *thing* for *chore*); and occasionally he lost meaning but did not stop to search for information (for example, *chore* for *chance*). He was able to demonstrate good retention of the important information in the text and to hypothesize as to why and how Vanessa changed.

In May of third grade, Henry's reading assessment indicated that he could read level N at an independent level and that his new instructional level was O. Henry started the year slightly above grade level, but was ending the year just on grade level. A look at rate and fluency indicate, however, that he could read faster and his phrasing and expression had improved. He read *The New Girl* (level O) at 97% accuracy—almost at the independent level—and had satisfactory comprehension. In Figure 70, you see the Bi-annual Assessment Summary form, which lets you look at Henry's progress over the year. He had achieved only one measured level of growth; however, when he began instruction in September, level N was slightly challenging for him, and at the end of

the year, level O was almost in the easy category. His teacher would have expected him to move quickly to level P.

Henry's reading assessment in September of grade 4 indicated that he had made progress over the summer. His independent reading level was P and his instructional level was Q, which was slightly challenging for him in terms of comprehension. In Figures 71 and 72, you see his Assessment Summary form and his instructional level Recording Form (*Not Too Cold for a Polar Bear*, level Q).

In addition, he had begun to read at a faster pace; however, his fluency rating did not increase, largely because Henry was beginning to read a little too fast for his processing system. An examination of the errors on *Not Too Cold for a Polar Bear* indicate that while his reading was 96% accurate, he did make careless mistakes and was not monitoring closely. He did, however, show excellent word-solving strategies. He was able to break the word apart by saying the first part of an unfamiliar word, and he sometimes reread to search for meaning. He was using all sources of information in a smoothly orchestrated way. His comprehension was satisfactory; however, he might have been relying on background knowledge of bears. For example, he stated that polar bears sleep in dens in the winter when the text clearly states that they stay awake. This is a relatively minor fact and did not mean his comprehension was poor; however, the teacher was concerned because Henry encountered the information during the silent part of his reading. This evidence might mean that Henry was not monitoring closely while reading silently.

In Figure 73, you see Henry's Assessment Summary Form for May of grade 4, and Figure 74 shows his reading record for the instructional level. He read level Q, *A Secret Home*, at 100% accuracy and at a very fast pace and satisfactory comprehension. His fluency rating, however, was only 1, mostly because Henry's reading sounded robotic and he was not noticing punctuation. His instructional level was R, *The Election,* and he achieved satisfactory comprehension but was again showing evidence of sliding over words rather than noticing errors, even when meaning was lost. His understanding of the text was only barely satisfactory. On the next level, his reading of *Amazing Animal Adaptations,* level S, was fairly accurate (91%) but with low comprehension and fluency.

In Figure 75, you can see Henry's Bi-annual Assessment Summary form.

In spring of grade 4, Henry began participation in daily small group guided reading, which continued until the second week of June. He also participated in a summer reading program in which he selected books of interest, and he resumed small-group instruction in September of his fifth-grade year. By the time his reading was assessed, he was reading level T independently and level U during instruction (see Figures 76 and 77).

Systems seem to be coming together for Henry. He was again reading right on grade level; he had slowed down a bit and was paying more attention to punctuation. His fluency rating was excellent again, as well as his comprehension. He was developing a real preference for informational texts!

In Figure 78, you see Henry's graph of reading progress for grades K–5. Like all other readers, Henry's path of progress is individual. Looking at it overall, he has made steady progress along a continuum of development. Sometimes the progress is very rapid, and at other times it seems to slow while, perhaps, some systems of strategies are being consolidated. The important thing is that he has continued to make progress and at the same time to enjoy texts of his own choosing for independent reading, as well as to participate in reading instruction at an appropriate level to support efficient processing.

Henry's Grade 3 September Assessment Conference

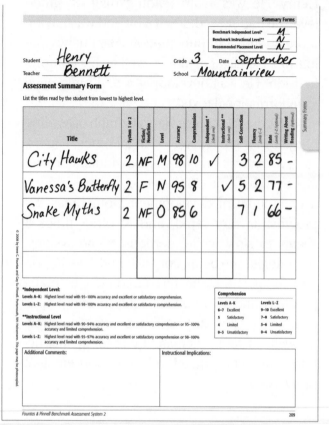

Figure 68. Henry's Assessment Summary Form, September, grade 3

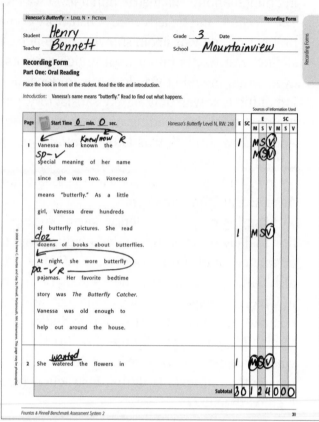

Figure 69a. Henry's Recording Form, *Vanessa's Butterfly*, level N

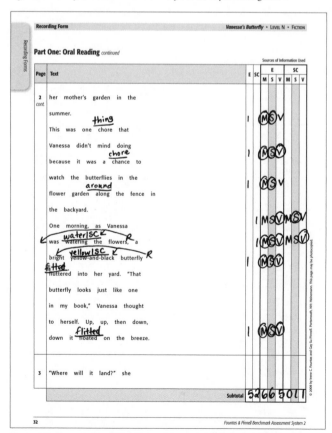

Figure 69b. Henry's Recording Form, *Vanessa's Butterfly*, level N

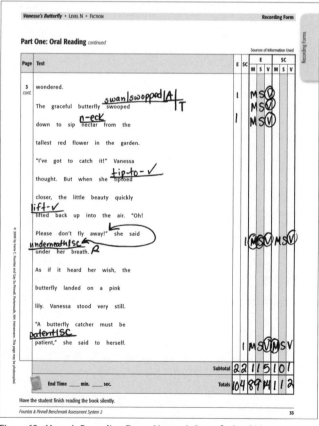

Figure 69c. Henry's Recording Form, *Vanessa's Butterfly*, level N

Henry's Grade 3 September Assessment Conference *(continued)* and Bi-Annual Assessment Summary

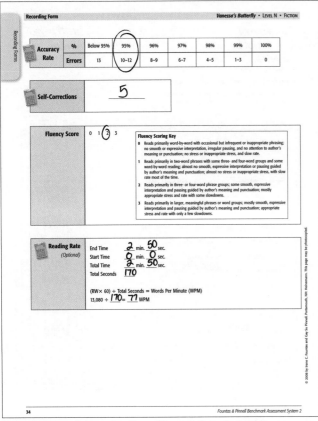

Figure 69d. Henry's Recording Form, *Vanessa's Butterfly*, level N

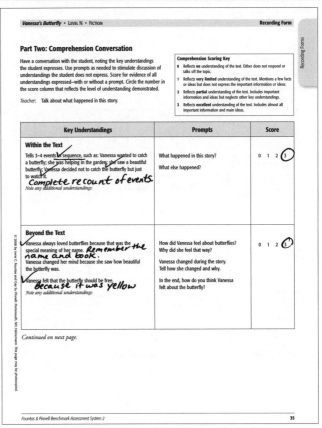

Figure 69e. Henry's Recording Form, *Vanessa's Butterfly*, level N

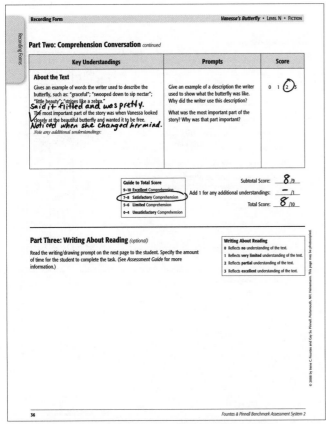

Figure 69f. Henry's Recording Form, *Vanessa's Butterfly*, level N

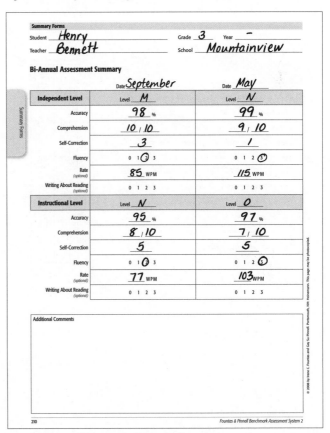

Figure 70. Henry's Bi-annual Assessment Summary

Henry's Grade 4 September Assessment Conference

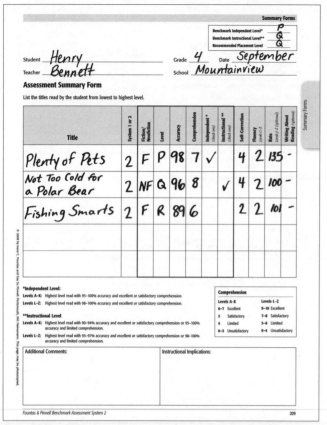

Figure 71. Henry's Assessment Summary form, September, grade 4

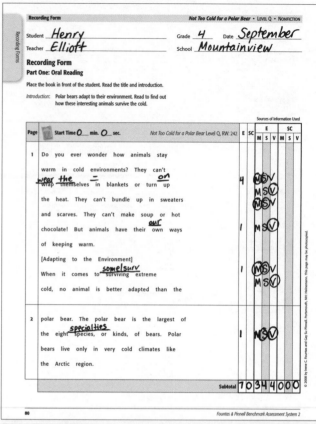

Figure 72a. Henry's Recording Form, *Not Too Cold for a Polar Bear*, level Q

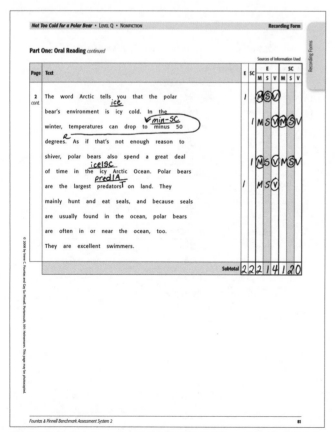

Figure 72b. Henry's Recording Form, *Not Too Cold for a Polar Bear*, level Q

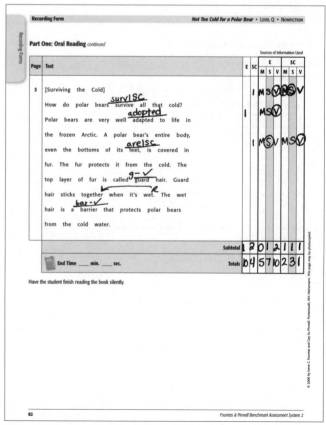

Figure 72c. Henry's Recording Form, *Not Too Cold for a Polar Bear*, level Q

Henry's Grade 4 September Assessment Conference *(continued)*

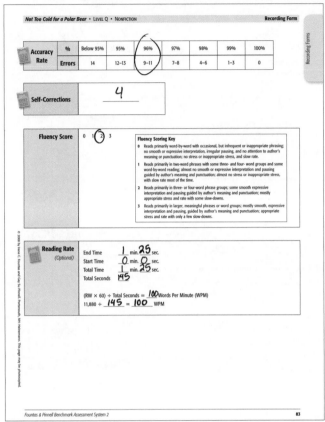

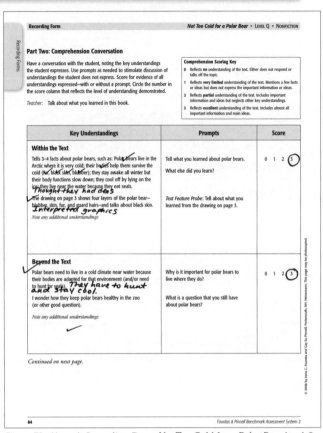

Figure 72d. Henry's Recording Form, *Not Too Cold for a Polar Bear,* level Q

Figure 72e. Henry's Recording Form, *Not Too Cold for a Polar Bear,* level Q

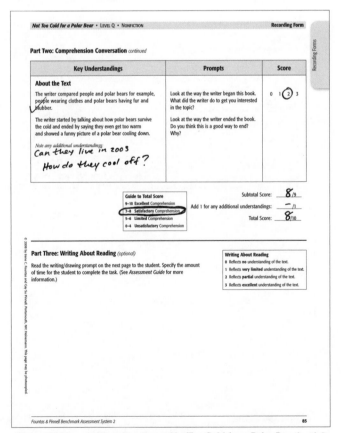

Figure 72f. Henry's Recording Form, *Not Too Cold for a Polar Bear,* level Q

Henry's Grade 4 May Assessment Conference

Figure 73. Henry's Assessment Summary form, May, grade 4

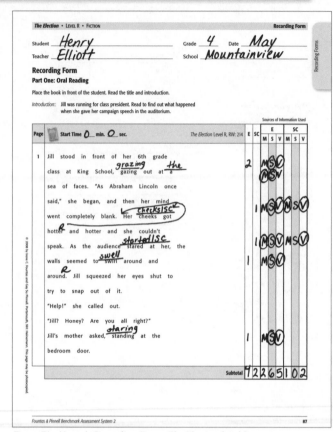

Figure 74a. Henry's Recording Form, *The Election*, level R

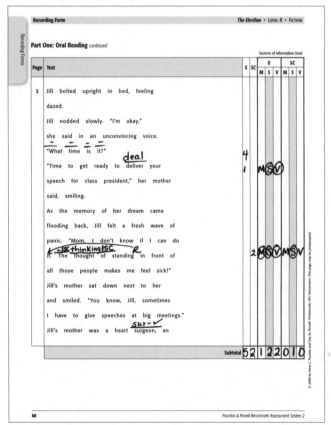

Figure 74b. Henry's Recording Form, *The Election*, level R

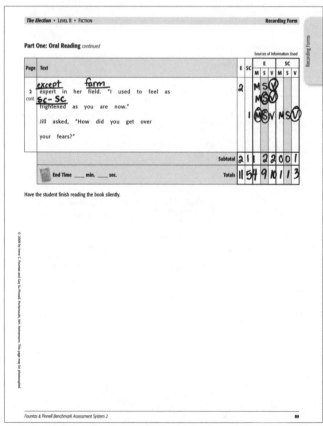

Figure 74c. Henry's Recording Form, *The Election*, level R

Henry's Grade 4 May Assessment Conference *(continued)*

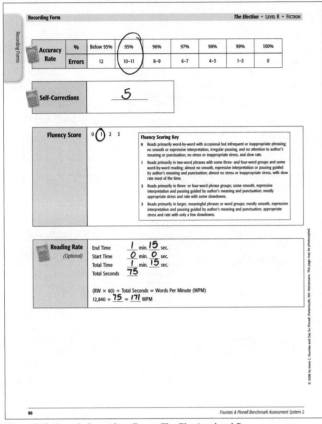

Figure 74d. Henry's Recording Form, *The Election*, level R

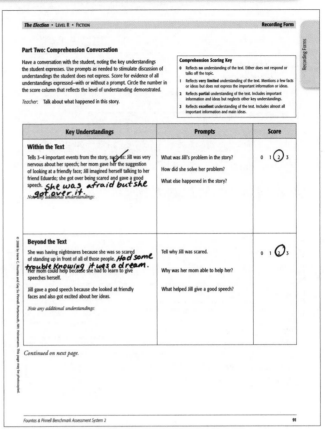

Figure 74e. Henry's Recording Form, *The Election*, level R

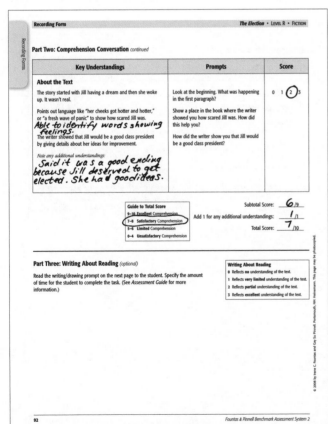

Figure 74f. Henry's Recording Form, *The Election*, level R

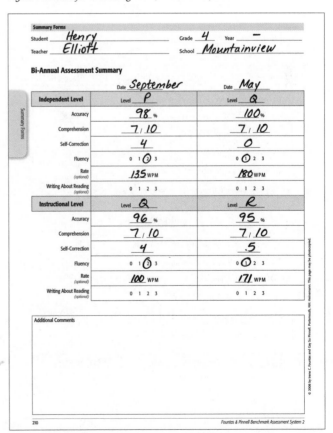

Figure 75. Henry's Bi-annual Assessment Summary

Henry's Grade 5 September Assessment Conference

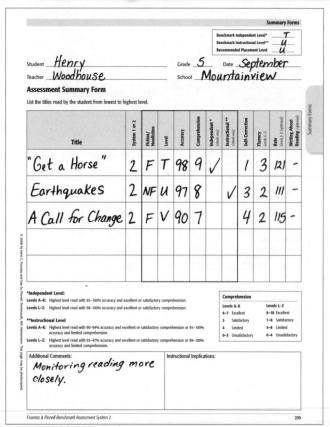

Figure 76. Henry's Assessment Summary Form, September, grade 5

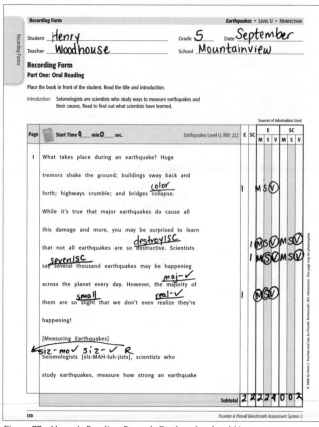

Figure 77a. Henry's Reading Record, *Earthquakes*, level U

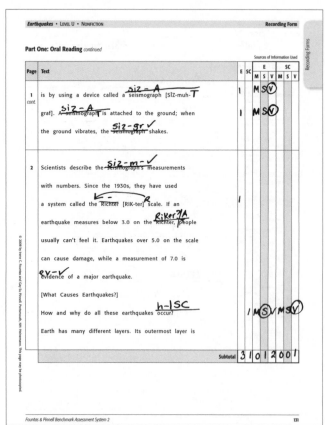

Figure 77b. Henry's Reading Record, *Earthquakes*, level U

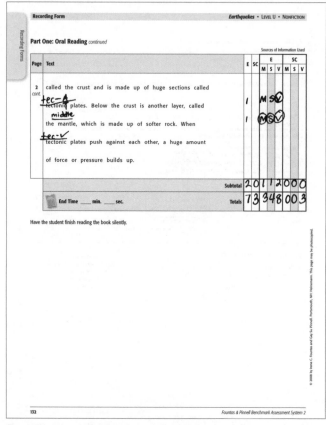

Figure 77c. Henry's Reading Record, *Earthquakes*, level U

Henry's Grade 5 September Assessment Conference and Longitudinal Record of Reading Progress

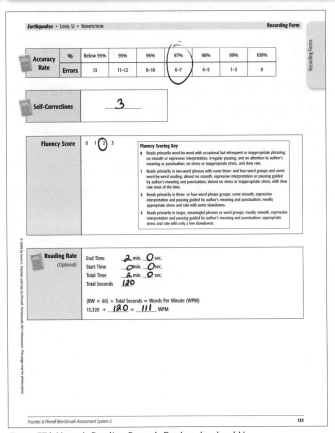

Figure 77d. Henry's Reading Record, *Earthquakes,* level U

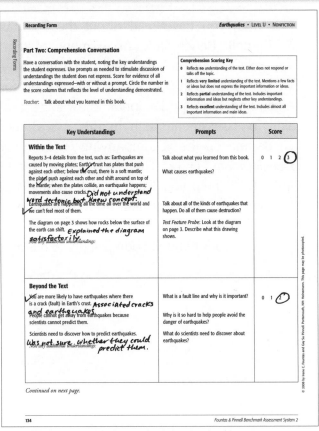

Figure 77e. Henry's Reading Record, *Earthquakes,* level U

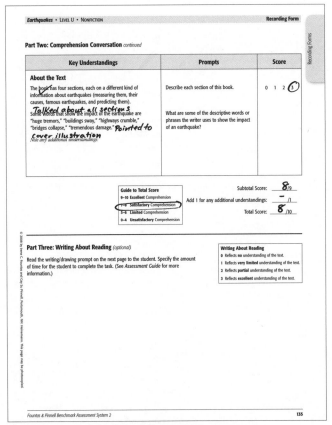

Figure 77f. Henry's Reading Record, *Earthquakes,* level U

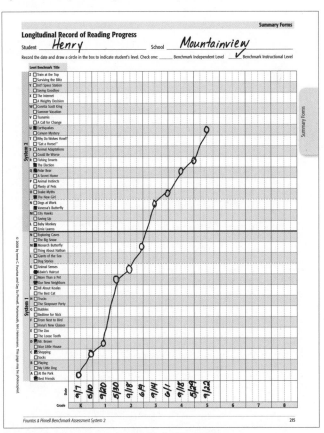

Figure 78. Henry's Longitudinal Record of Reading Progress

Professional Development Options

Now that you have read about the Fountas & Pinnell Benchmark Assessment System, you can further enhance your learning in a variety of ways. In your kit are critical tools for extending your professional knowledge and skill in assessment, both in this *Assessment Guide* and on the accompanying *Professional Development* DVD. The DVD offers many features to help you learn how to administer the Benchmark Assessment from beginning to end. The tutorial with practice sessions allows you to try your hand at coding specific reading behaviors after viewing model demonstrations. Examples of oral readings and comprehension conversations at different levels can help to build knowledge and broaden your experience as you practice your assessment skills. Using it with colleagues is a good way to ensure that all teachers in your building are also working with consistent guidelines. You can also log onto the fountasandpinnellbenchmarkassessment.com website to learn about in-person seminars at your school or district as well as to get ongoing information and updates related to your Fountas & Pinnell Benchmark Assessment System.

Appendices

Appendix A contains detailed descriptions of critical features in the Benchmark books.

Appendix B contains a brief description and table of contents for the *Benchmark Assessment Forms* book and CD-ROM.

Appendix C describes the *Data Management* CD-ROM.

Appendix D describes the *Professional Development* DVD

Frequently Asked Questions

Glossary

Appendix A: Benchmark Books

Benchmark books are the centerpiece of the Benchmark Assessment System. They provide the material for the student's oral reading from which the teacher observes many dimensions of reading behavior. In System 2, there are thirty books, fifteen fiction and fifteen nonfiction, ranging from level L, the easiest, to level Z, the hardest. System 2 provides one fiction and one nonfiction book at each level.

Each fiction and nonfiction book has been written and edited to represent the designated Fountas and Pinnell level. Each represents the specific characteristics of that level. You can find very detailed analyses of texts at each level of the gradient, A–Z, in *Leveled Books for Readers, K–8: Matching Texts to Readers* *for Effective Teaching* (Heinemann, 2006) and *The Continuum of Literacy Learning: A Guide for Teaching K–8* (Heinemann, 2008).

In this section, we briefly describe the thirty benchmark books. If you look at the lists in bullets, you will see some important descriptions of each book. These characteristics emerged from analyzing the text to place it on the gradient. They are descriptions of what makes the book easier or harder and are related to the *demands* the text makes on the reader. Reading these descriptions will help you realize what the reader has to do to read the book. If the reader is successful, then you have good evidence that he or she can meet the demands of texts on the level.

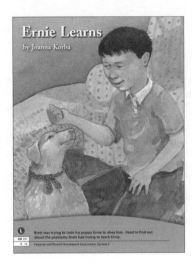

dog what to do. He tried to remember more and then decided to start. Maybe that was all.

"Sit, Ernie!" Brett said.

He nudged the puppy, and the little dog sat.

Then Brett made another attempt. But Ernie just looked at him. Then Brett showed the puppy over and over how to sit. Again, Ernie forgot what to do.

"Maybe you don't like sitting," Brett said. "Let's try something new." He backed away from his dog. "Stay!" he said.

Ernie didn't stay. He didn't lie down. And he didn't come when he was called.

Brett's mom was watching from the porch. Brett yelled, "Mom, why can't I teach Ernie anything?"

"I think you forgot an important step," Mom said. She held out some puppy treats. "You have to make him want to be good! Watch for him to do something right. Then praise him and reward him. That's how Dad and I get you to be good!" ■

Brett grinned and said, "Aw, you know I'd be good anyway!" Mom laughed. "Puppies and people aren't all that different,"

Ernie Learns

Fiction level L
Total words: 324
Average sentence length: 6.8 words

In this story, Brett tries to train his puppy Ernie to obey him. He tries telling Ernie what to do, but nothing works. His mom suggests praising and rewarding Ernie, just like she and Dad do to get Brett to be good. The puppy treats do the trick. The story ends with Brett giving his mom a "happy bark."

Text characteristics:

▸ variation in sentence length with some sentences over fifteen words long

▸ mostly one- and two-syllable words

▸ dialogue, both simple and split, between two speakers

▸ simple story line

▸ paragraphs, marked by indentation

▸ play on language at the end

The baby grabs the fur on his mother's belly and begins to feed. The baby is snug against his mother's warm body. Later, the baby curls his long tail, arms, and legs around his mother.

The First Weeks

For a few weeks, the baby rides on his mother's back. The mother carries, feeds, and grooms her baby. She keeps the baby safe from snakes, hawks, and big cats.

Sometimes, the baby monkey loses his grip and falls to the rain forest floor. A monkey from the troop climbs down the tree and

A baby capuchin clings to his mother's back.

picks up the baby. Back with his mother, the baby hangs on again.

After a month, the baby begins to learn about the world. He moves away from his mother. But he only goes as far as his tail will let him! The baby holds on to his mother using his long tail.

Caring for the baby is hard work! Other monkeys in the troop

Hang On, Baby Monkey

Nonfiction level L

Total words: 285

Average sentence length: 10.6 words

This text provides information about how a monkey troop takes care of their young. The text is presented in three sections in temporal sequence, with headings. Each section tells about a part of the baby monkey's life. An important main idea is that the monkeys in a troop help each other as members of a family would. The baby monkey survives by hanging on to his mother; he rides on his mother's back at first and then stays close to her by holding on with his tail.

Text characteristics:

▶ three sections with headings

▶ told in temporal sequence

▶ monkey troop compared to family

▶ themes of survival and animals depending on each other

▶ varied sentence length, most ten to twelve words long

▶ simple words, mostly two syllables

▶ paragraphs set off by indentation

▶ photographs with captions

▶ map with legend

▶ glossary

was responsible enough to get a dog.

"Great! How can I prove I'm responsible? I'll do anything!"

"First, you should call the animal shelter and ask them how much it costs to get a dog. Then you'll have to save the money."

"I can certainly do that!" I said.

I called the shelter. I found out it costs one hundred and forty dollars to get a puppy and seventy dollars to get a dog. I decided to get a grown dog!

How long would it take me to save seventy dollars? I started to do the math.

My allowance was seven dollars a

week, if I did all my chores. I never used to save any of it. Now I'd have to save a whole lot. ■

With seven dollars a week, I'd have seventy dollars in ten weeks. But that was too long to wait!

I asked Mom about doing some extra jobs for her. She agreed to pay me three dollars for each one. She said I could clean the garage, vacuum the car, paint the kitchen door, brush all the cobwebs out of the basement (yuck!) . . .

"Okay, Mom, I think that's enough for now!" I said.

The next few weeks were really hard. I did all my chores, even

2

3

Saving Up

Fiction level M
Total words: 394
Average sentence length: 8.6 words

Danny wants to get a dog, but he has to prove to his mom that he is responsible. He undertakes two responsibilities: finding out how much a dog would cost, and earning the money. Danny meets his goal by doing extra chores and saving the seventy dollars. He names his new dog Buck.

Text characteristics:

- ▶ straightforward story told in chronological sequence
- ▶ told in first-person narrative
- ▶ dialogue between two characters, some unassigned
- ▶ mostly simple or compound sentences
- ▶ some strings of verb clauses set off by commas
- ▶ joke at the end
- ▶ full range of punctuation, including dashes
- ▶ humor at the end

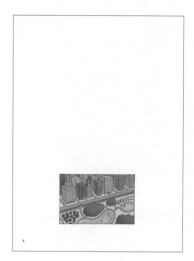
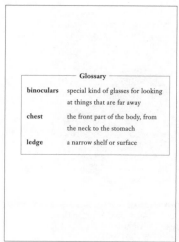

City Hawks

Nonfiction level M
Total words: 315
Average sentence length: 9.4 words

This book tells the story of Pale Male, a red-tailed hawk who built a nest on the ledge of a fancy apartment building across from Central Park in New York City. The hawk found a mate and raised several families, in the process becoming famous. A controversy arose when people living in the building got tired of being watched by people with binoculars. The nest was taken down, but marching protesters soon had it up again for good. Information is organized into three sections with headings. Drawings and photographs are included.

Text characteristics:

▶ organized into three sections with headings, in chronological order

▶ journalistic style with a summary lead

▶ presentation of two perspectives: people who live in the building and do not want others observing them and people who want Pale Male to have his nest

▶ author's perspective supporting Pale Male

▶ mostly simple or compound sentences

▶ mostly one- or two-syllable words

▶ no technical vocabulary

▶ glossary

She watered the flowers in her mother's garden in the summer.

This was one chore that Vanessa didn't mind doing because it was a chance to watch the butterflies in the flower garden along the fence in the backyard.

One morning, as Vanessa was watering the flowers, a bright yellow-and-black butterfly fluttered into her yard. "That butterfly looks just like one in my book," Vanessa thought to herself. Up, up, then down, down it floated on the breeze.

"Where will it land?" she wondered.

The graceful butterfly swooped down to sip nectar from the tallest red flower in the garden. "I've got to catch it!" Vanessa thought. But when she tiptoed closer, the little beauty quickly lifted back up into the air. "Oh! Please don't fly away!" she said under her breath.

As if it heard her wish, the butterfly landed on a pink lily. Vanessa stood very still. "A butterfly catcher must be patient," she said to herself. ■

Vanessa's Butterfly

Fiction level N

Total words: 299

Average sentence length: 9.9 words

Vanessa, whose name means "butterfly," loves butterflies. She studies them and loves to watch them in her flower garden. One day Vanessa sees a beautiful yellow-and-black butterfly and wants to catch it. The more she watches it, the more she appreciates its beauty. Realizing that the butterfly needs to be free, Vanessa decides to be a butterfly watcher instead of a butterfly catcher.

Text characteristics:

▶ story lead providing background to support Vanessa's love of butterflies

▶ foreshadowing of the end with the information that her favorite story was *The Butterfly Catcher*

▶ descriptive language showing the butterfly's movement (*floated on the breeze, swooped*)

▶ character development (Vanessa's change of mind)

▶ some long sentences with twenty or more words

▶ mostly one- and two-syllable words

What Are Guide Dogs?

Guide dogs help blind people get from place to place and lead independent lives. With a guide dog, blind people can go to the grocery store, ride the bus, or take a trip on a plane. Guide dogs are allowed in places where most other dogs are not.

Not just any dog can be a guide dog. A guide dog needs many months of training at a special school.

At school they learn to behave quietly, especially in public. Guide dogs have to focus on helping their owners. They are taught to ignore other things, such as interesting smells and other animals.

Guide dogs help their owners cross streets safely.

They also learn to keep still and quiet in busy places, such as shopping malls or offices. Most dogs would have a very hard time doing that!

Dogs At Work

If you see a guide dog doing its job, remember not to pet or talk to it. Guiding is very hard to do. It requires a dog's full attention. ■

A guide dog wears a special harness, called a lead harness.

Dogs at Work

Nonfiction level N
Total words: 306
Average sentence length: 11.4 words

This book explains the role of guide dogs in helping blind people. The text includes an introduction and two sections with headings. An important main idea is that guide dogs require special training. Photographs with captions and a glossary are included.

Text characteristics:

▶ starts with a question that compares guide dogs to best friends

▶ details what guide dogs know how to do

▶ provides a special meaning for the word *independent*

▶ most sentences ten to twenty words

▶ some technical vocabulary such as *harness* and *handler*

▶ photographs with captions

▶ glossary

A month later, Nora walked into her new school. Her sneakers squeaked on the shiny, polished floors. She was not surprised that the other kids turned, stared, and whispered, but didn't say hello. "No one ever talks to the new girl," she told herself.

At lunch, Nora looked around the crowded cafeteria. At every table kids were eating lunch with their special friends, talking and laughing. No kids invited Nora to sit with them. Only one girl smiled at Nora. She was sitting by herself looking lonely and nervous. "She's probably new, too," Nora thought, so she just ignored her. Nora dreamed of being in a group of friends, just as she was in her old school.

That night she told her mother about her terrible day. "Did you talk to anyone?" her mother asked. Nora shook her head. "All the kids ignored me." ■

"I'm sorry, honey," Mom said. "But remember, to get you have to give." She was always coming up with sayings that sounded like they belonged on bumper stickers. "There must be one other kid at your school who could use a friend," Mom added. "Maybe you should try making the first move."

The next day Nora saw the girl who had smiled at her the day before. This time Nora smiled back, and before long they were talking. The girl's name was Liz, and this was her seventh school in five years. She was an Army kid, too!

The New Girl

Fiction level O
Total words: 402
Average sentence length: 9.0 words

Nora's mom is in the Army, and Nora is unhappy because her family has to move again. The first day at her new school is difficult. The only friendly person is another girl, who smiles at her, but Nora ignores her. When she returns home, her mother advises her that "to get you have to give." Nora follows this advice and makes a friend of the other new girl, also an Army kid.

Text characteristics:

- ▶ assumption of background information (military families moving)
- ▶ setting requiring inference (feeling of a newcomer) and understanding of the importance of peer group
- ▶ some two-syllable words
- ▶ some adjectives in strings, set off by commas
- ▶ most sentences complex (with at least two clauses)
- ▶ variety in vocabulary related to dialogue (*grumbled, complained*)
- ▶ dialogue among three characters
- ▶ simple foreshadowing
- ▶ passage of time
- ▶ meaning of slogans or "sayings"
- ▶ character development (learning a simple lesson)

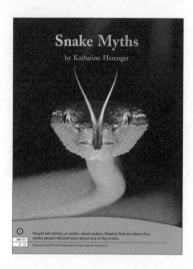

Snakes' eyes are protected by a layer of clear scales.

Myth 2

Snakes' tongues are not dangerous. That's another misunderstanding. In fact, only a snake's fangs are harmful. A snake flicks its tongue to smell the air. It can use smells to figure out which way its prey is moving or whether an enemy is near. If a snake flicks its tongue at you, it's just trying to figure out if you're something good to eat. (Don't worry—snakes rarely eat people!)

Poisonous snakes have two large fangs in the upper front part of the mouth.

Myth 3

Some people think that snakes feel wet and slimy. But a snake's skin is really very dry and smooth. This smoothness makes a snake's skin look shiny and wet. The way a snake's scales move, sliding along the ground, may also make them look slimy. ■

Myth 4

Snakes can bend and twist and slither and slide this way and that. Many people think they have no bones. But snakes do

Snake Myths

Nonfiction level O
Total words: 337
Average sentence length: 10.2 words

This book introduces five commonly held myths about snakes: (1) snakes hypnotize their prey; (2) snakes' tongues are dangerous; (3) snakes feel wet and slimy; (4) snakes have no bones; and (5) most snakes are poisonous. Each myth is introduced, then the evidence to the contrary is presented. The main idea of the text is that snakes do not want to harm people.

Text characteristics:

▶ introduction provides the main idea of the book

▶ information organized into five myths and a conclusion

▶ clear organization within sections—presentation of myth first, followed by evidence to the contrary

▶ photographs with captions

▶ some three- and four-syllable words (*fascination*, *hypnotize*)

▶ vocabulary (such as *myth*) defined within the text

▶ parenthetical material set off by commas in a few sentences

▶ glossary

Plenty of Pets
by Stephanie Herbek

The bell rang, and Nate grabbed his backpack and headed home in a downpour. His neighbor, Mrs. Gonzalez, pulled up beside him in her minivan. "Hop in," she said. "It's a deluge out there!" Even before the door closed, Nate's nose started to tickle.

"Achoo!" he sneezed loudly. "Achoo! Achoo!" Rubbing his red, itchy eyes, Nate croaked, "Is there an animal in here?"

"Just Daisy!" Mrs. Gonzalez said sheepishly, as a pudgy bulldog poked its head over the front seat. Nate walked home.

A sniffling Nate woke up Saturday morning feeling sorry for himself. "Why do I have to be allergic to everything?" he fretted as he trudged downstairs.

His mom smiled. "I have exciting news!" she exclaimed. "My friend Dr. Hung, who works at the aquarium, could use your help with the animals on Saturdays. How about it?" ◼

"Thanks, Mom, but the idea of sneezing all day doesn't appeal to me," said Nate.

"You're allergic to animals that have fur or feathers," Mom pointed out, "not to marine animals that live in the water."

Nate felt nervous as they drove to the aquarium, but after he met Dr. Hung, his anxiety melted away. Within minutes, they were standing next to a huge saltwater pool. "Meet our Pacific white-sided dolphins, Nate," said Dr. Hung. "They're ready for their lunch!"

Dr. Hung handed Nate a pair of floppy rubber gloves and a heavy pail

2

3

Plenty of Pets

Fiction level P
Total words: 404
Average sentence length: 9.0 words

Nate is disappointed that he can't bring home his classroom's hamster because he is allergic to everything with fur or feathers. His mom arranges for him to help Dr. Hung in the aquarium on Saturday and he discovers that dolphins, especially one named Splash, will eat from his hand. He has a wonderful time. When he gets home, another surprise is waiting. His mom gives him a pet fish, which he names Little Splash.

Text characteristics:

▶ varied sentence length, with some sentences fifteen to twenty words

▶ many complex sentences

▶ divided dialogue

▶ mostly familiar vocabulary, with a few difficult words such as *sheepishly*, *beluga*, *fretted*, and *sneeze-free* (coined for humor)

▶ straightforward story with clear problem and resolution

▶ third-person narrative

▶ words to signal passage of time: *later*, *after*, day of the week

▶ little or no character development

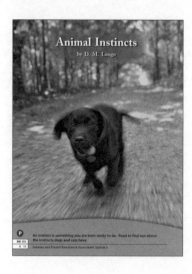

seem odd to us. Yet our family pets are behaving in exactly the same way as their ancestors did thousands of years ago.

The Pack Is Back

The dogs you know are probably household pets and live indoors. Wild dogs live in packs—groups in which animals live, work, and hunt together. Dogs in a pack depend on one another to survive, so pack instinct is very strong. The leader of the pack is the smartest dog. The other dogs in the pack obey the leader. This instinct is one reason that pet dogs are such devoted family members. Dogs regard their human families as their packs

and one family member as the leader of the pack. ■

Sebastian is a pet dog. Why does he enjoy chasing cars? He is following his predator instinct. A predator is an animal that hunts for its food. Like a predator, Sebastian runs after anything that moves quickly, like a rabbit—or a car!

Dogs love to run.

Animal Instincts

Nonfiction level P
Total words: 344
Average sentence length: 10.4 words

Focusing on cats and dogs, this text explains the origins of some common behaviors of these pets. Belonging to a "pack," for example, makes dogs devoted family members, and their predator instinct leads them to chase cars. Cats pounce on anything that moves because of the instinctual behavior of hunting. The text is presented with an introduction and three sections with headings.

Text characteristics:

▶ comparison of animal and human instinctual behaviors

▶ some technical terms (*instinctual, instinct, pack, predator*) all defined within the text

▶ examples to illustrate points

▶ photograph with caption

▶ glossary

As they followed the winding trails, Aunt Maddy pointed out all kinds of plants and wildlife. They stopped for a water break. Then Lenny shouted, "Look out for the spider!" and Beth froze. It was obvious to Aunt Maddy that the kids were scared of spiders.

"Has a spider ever harmed either of you?" Aunt Maddy asked. Both kids shook their heads. "Sounds like you suffer from arachnophobia (uh RAK nuh FOE bee uh)—an extreme fear of spiders."

"Aren't spiders dangerous?" Lenny asked. "I heard about a boy who got really sick from a spider bite."

Aunt Maddy nodded. "Sure, some spiders, like the black widow, are dangerous." ∎

"Yes," Lenny said excitedly, "that's the kind that bit that boy."

"Well," Aunt Maddy replied, "you'd certainly want to avoid black widows, but most spiders won't hurt you. They want to avoid you as much as you want to avoid them."

They walked for a while, and then Aunt Maddy stopped. "Take a look down there," she said, gesturing toward the ground.

Beth and Lenny stared downward but didn't see anything except dirt and a few small rocks. They stood very still for a few minutes, and along came a furry spider about the size of a quarter. Aunt Maddy whispered, "That's a trap-door spider. Don't worry. It won't hurt you at all."

As the three of them watched, the spider used its two front legs to flip open a small, perfectly formed trap door in the earth. The spider then disappeared under the ground, pulling the door shut behind it. Beth

A Secret Home

Fiction level Q
Total words: 481
Average sentence length: 9.4 words

Lenny and Beth go with their Aunt Maddy on a lengthy hike through a dusty canyon. Both children are afraid of spiders and have some misconceptions about them. Aunt Maddy points out an interesting spider, the trap-door, and the children become so interested in it that they overcome their fear.

Text characteristics:

▸ foreshadowing of an "adventure" in the opening paragraph

▸ some very short sentences in the dialogue; most sentences ten to twenty words

▸ technical word, *arachnophobia*, with pronunciation guide in parentheses

▸ content information about spiders

▸ character development as shown by children's becoming interested in spiders

▸ turning point on page 4 when children become interested in the trap-door spider

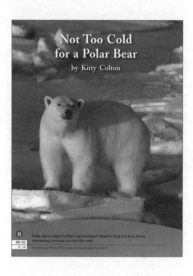

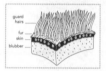

Not Too Cold for a Polar Bear

Nonfiction level Q

Total words: 386

Average sentence length: 12.5 words

An opening question frames the central idea of this text—that some animals have ways of surviving very cold weather. The book focuses on how polar bears are adapted to live in the Arctic region. Organized into two sections, the text provides specific details about how the characteristics of the polar bear's body work together to provide protection. It ends on a humorous note by showing how polar bears cool off when they get too hot.

Text characteristics:

 ▶ opens with posing a question

 ▶ two sections with headings

 ▶ first section with general information about polar bears
   and their environment

 ▶ second section with specific details about the polar bear's body

 ▶ technical vocabulary (for example, *guard hair, blubber*)

 ▶ variable sentence length but some with over twenty words

 ▶ photographs with captions

 ▶ drawing with cutaway of skin

 ▶ glossary

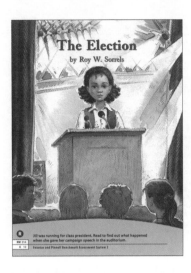

Jill bolted upright in bed, feeling dazed.

Jill nodded slowly. "I'm okay," she said in an unconvincing voice. "What time is it?"

"Time to get ready to deliver your speech for class president," her mother said, smiling.

As the memory of her dream came flooding back, Jill felt a fresh wave of panic. "Mom, I don't know if I can do it. The thought of standing in front of all those people makes me feel sick!"

Jill's mother sat down next to her and smiled. "You know, Jill, sometimes I have to give speeches at big meetings." Jill's mother was a heart surgeon, an expert in her field. "I used to feel as frightened as you are now."

Jill asked, "How did you get over your fears?" ∎

"Well," her mother began, "when I have to get up in front of hundreds of strangers, I focus on one friendly face I know. Then I imagine that the two of us are sitting across a table from each other and talking about work."

"And do you stop being scared?"

"Well, not completely. It's normal to feel nervous about something that's new to you. But if you can find the courage to do it anyway, it won't feel so scary the next time. You can do it—I'm sure of it."

Later that morning, Jill walked slowly across the auditorium stage and stood behind the podium. She took a deep breath and scanned the faces in the crowd. There, in the second row, was her friend Eduardo. He smiled at her encouragingly. Jill imagined herself talking directly to Eduardo, exactly as her mother had suggested.

The Election

Fiction level R
Total words: 492
Average sentence length: 11.1 words

This story begins with a dream in which Jill is speaking to her sixth-grade class and draws a blank. As she jolts awake, she realizes that she is afraid to speak to her class as a candidate for class president. Her mother gives her some good advice (looking for one friendly face). Jill tries the technique, relaxes, and feels very good by the end of the speech.

Text characteristics:

▶ requires reader to understand that the first paragraph was only a dream

▶ requires understanding of the setting and its contribution to the character's feelings

▶ mostly familiar vocabulary with a few difficult words (*podium*, *unconvincing*)

▶ most sentences between ten and twenty words

▶ full range of punctuation including dash and ellipses

▶ description of internal feelings of the central character and how and why they change

▶ requires reader to infer why Jill would be a good president and to predict the outcomes of the election

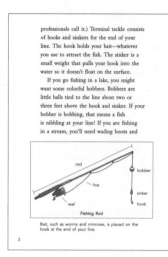

Fishing Smarts

Nonfiction level R
Total words: 505
Average sentence length: 11.7 words

The important idea in this book—that fishing is more complicated than it appears—is introduced in the first paragraph. The text has three sections with headings. Information about equipment and supplies is presented in the first two sections. In the last section, there is a response to the superstitions surrounding fishing, which were introduced in section two. The text ends with an implicit suggestion to "catch and release" the fish.

Text characteristics:

▶ technical words, most of which are defined within the text (*tackle, reel, spool, terminal tackle, hooks and sinkers, bobber, sinker*)

▶ familiar vocabulary

▶ requires understanding of the context

▶ requires understanding of the historical reference to superstitions in the 1700s

▶ information on equipment and supplies in the first two sections

▶ information about fishing "know-how" in the third section

▶ implicit suggestion to "catch and release" fish

▶ photographs with captions

▶ diagram of fishing rod with labels

▶ glossary

"How 'bout you?" I casually asked.
"Already ate," he answered, just as casually.

He lied to me, and I lied to him. Ever since Dad lost his job and the money dried up, we lied and kept secrets. The façade helps us make it easier for each other.

Effortlessly, I told another one. "Dad? Anthony asked me to stay over again. OK?"

"An opportunity to sleep in a bed? Go for it." ■

Not to mention a home-cooked supper and breakfast. It was easier for Dad, too. Then he didn't have to feed me.

"Heads up!" said Dad. He lobbed over a brown bag. In the bag was my standard lunch: a peanut-butter sandwich and an apple.

"Thanks," I said as I hopped on my bike. Dad told me where he'd be job-hunting that day, in case I needed him. "Come here right after school tomorrow," he said. "It's moving day." To be as inconspicuous as possible, we moved the van a lot.

I had an unauthorized stop to make on the way to school—one of those secrets I mentioned earlier. Dad didn't know that every Tuesday morning I earned a couple of bucks unloading produce behind Cardozo's Market. I used the money for school supplies that I couldn't bear to ask my dad to buy.

I worked for twenty minutes before I got up the nerve to ask, "Mr. Cardozo . . . I was wondering. Any chance you could hire me permanently?"

"I wish I could, Ray, but what I really need is a full-time produce manager. If you were older and out of school . . . " He shook his head sympathetically.

I got things settled with Anthony. Then all through math I thought about that job at Cardozo's. So during lunch period, I hand-lettered a flyer:

HELP WANTED
PRODUCE MANAGER
CARDOZO'S MARKET
THIRD AND CENTRAL PARKWAY

Could Be Worse

Fiction level S
Total words: 589
Average sentence length: 9.6 words

This book tells the story of Ray and his father, who are homeless. Ray's father is unemployed, and they live in a battered van. The story begins with the retelling of a joke about a man for whom everything goes wrong. He says, "It could be worse. At least it's not raining." Just then, it starts to pour. This joke is important because it represents Ray's and his dad's life at this point. They don't have enough money even to eat, but they both lie—putting on a good face, each to the other. Ray takes action against his problem by working a few hours in a market. Learning that the market needs a full-time produce manager, Ray finds a way to let his dad know. His dad gets the job. At the end, Ray's dad says, "It's not going to make us millionaires. But it could be worse." This comment echoes back to the joke at the beginning, but this time, it isn't raining.

Text characteristics:

▶ begins and ends with reference to the joke, "It could be worse . . ."

▶ first-person narrative

▶ varied sentence length, some very short, but several more than twenty words long

▶ wide range of punctuation, including semicolon and ellipses

▶ mostly familiar vocabulary but several difficult words (*unauthorized, permanently, opportunity, professional*)

▶ use of rain as a symbol of trouble

▶ requires understanding that Ray and his dad lied to protect each other

▶ requires understanding of the setting

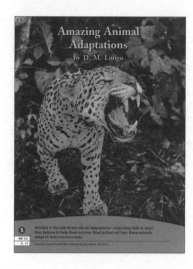

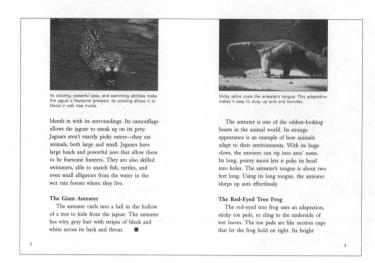

Amazing Animal Adaptations

Nonfiction level S
Total words: 407
Average sentence length: 14.2 words

This highly descriptive text provides information about how animals in the rain forest environment behave in ways that allow them to survive. The information is presented in five sections. The beginning is a suspenseful description of a jaguar, an anteater, and a red-eyed tree frog going about their night lives. The three following sections provide details about each of the three animals. The text is written in present tense. The important idea is summarized in the last section—that all living things are adapted to their environments.

Text characteristics:

▶ introduces the main idea with a description of the three animals going about their nocturnal lives

▶ details on the three animals in three sections

▶ summarizes the main idea at the end

▶ key vocabulary words related to the concept (*adaptation, camouflage, environment, predators*)

▶ varied sentence length, with most between ten and twenty words

▶ photographs with captions

▶ glossary

"Get a Horse!"

Fiction level T
Total words: 551
Average sentence length: 12.5 words

The story takes place in 1904, when Henry Ford's automobile was a new invention and many people ridiculed the horseless carriage. In the beginning of the story, Ethan is embarrassed when his father drives a Model A home. After riding in it, however, Ethan decides that he likes going as fast as 20 miles an hour. After his worries about Chester, the aging horse owned by the family, are alleviated, Ethan asks for another ride.

Text characteristics:

▶ requires understanding of the setting and attitudes of people at the time

▶ character change in attitude

▶ requires reader to infer Ethan's feelings and the reasons for them (initial embarrassment and worry about Chester the horse)

▶ words like *trousers* and *carriage* that are not commonly used today and/or had different meanings in 1904

▶ descriptive words

▶ varied sentence length, with some complex sentences of more than twenty words

Types of Howls

There are several types of wolf howls, each with its own particular purpose. The most common howl is a loud, deep call that can be heard up to ten miles away, depending on the weather. The purpose of this type of howl is to unite the pack. The wolves within a pack are usually related, and the average-sized pack is eight to fifteen wolves. Sometimes, while hunting, one or more pack members may become separated from the rest of the group. A chorus of wolves may howl to help the lost wolves get back to the family. ■

Get the Facts About Wolves	
Average Length (from nose to tail tip)	females: 4½–6 ft. males: 5–6½ ft.
Average Height (to the shoulder)	26–32 inches
Average Weight	females: 60–80 lbs. males: 70–110 lbs.
Weight at Birth	1 lb.
Fur Color	grey; sometimes also black or white
Food	deer, moose, elk, bison, beaver

Reasons for Howls

It's common for wolves to howl before setting out to hunt for food. The purpose of this howl may be to excite pack members and help them bond. It's as if they are a team preparing to compete. But once the hunt starts, the wolves are silent. Howling during a hunt would only alert the potential prey that it is in danger.

The howling begins again after a successful hunt. These howls seem to sound satisfied! Again, it's as if the wolf team has just scored a major victory!

Wolves communicate not only within a pack, but between packs as well. Packs can howl back and forth for hours. This may be their way of defending their territory from neighboring packs. These howls warn other packs to keep their distance.

Wolves also howl when they feel lonely or isolated, or are seeking mates. This type of howl has a different sound; it rises and falls, dragging out at the end.

Even six-month-old wolf pups know where, when, and to whom they should howl.

2   3

Why Do Wolves Howl?

Nonfiction level T
Total words: 523
Average sentence length: 13.8 words

This text describes wolves' howls as a kind of language that they use to communicate with each other. After an introduction that outlines the misconceptions about wolves, the information is presented in three sections: (1) types of howls; (2) reasons for howls; and (3) howls are unique. It seems that wolves' howls may be used to identify one another. No two wolves within a pack howl on the same note at the same time.

Text characteristics:

> ▶ begins with contrasting misconceptions about the real reasons wolves howl

> ▶ information presented with an introduction and three sections with headings

> ▶ varied sentence length with most between ten and twenty words

> ▶ many different words to describe wolves' howls

> ▶ ending paragraph referring back to beginning

> ▶ chart providing general facts about wolves (information not in the body of the text)

> ▶ photographs with captions

> ▶ glossary

Canyon Mystery
by Laura Shallop

Marta and her curious dog Sniffles are exploring a canyon in a New Mexico desert. Read to find out what Sniffles and Marta discover.

Fountas and Pinnell Benchmark Assessment System 2

Soon, Marta reaches her favorite lookout at the summit of a high mesa. She spots a majestic golden eagle that is circling overhead, high above the valley. The sun on her face is a constant reminder that the desert will be sweltering soon. She checks her watch, then tells Sniffles, "It's time to head home, boy." As they make their careful way back downhill, the eagle lets out a screech in the silent blue sky. Warily, Marta stops and searches the desert below. ◼

Sniffles turns to stare at Redcliff Mountain towering behind them. Without warning, the hound dashes uphill. "Sniffles, come back!" Marta calls out, but her dog has vanished into the hillside.

More apprehensive than angry, Marta checks her watch again and sets off to search for her pet. She backtracks to the spot where the trail splits. One path twists up the steep, jagged sides of Eagle Rock Canyon while the other disappears into a tangled patch of needle-sharp cacti. Marta's watch reads 8:00 a.m. The temperature is climbing, and the air is hot, dry, and still.

"Sniiiiffles! Where aaaare you?" Marta calls.

This time, she hears her dog barking from a cliff about twenty yards up the canyon. "Come down here, Sniffles!" she yells. "It's getting late!"

The hound is barking furiously now. "What is it, boy?" Marta asks with a shaky voice, as she climbs the wind-worn slope apprehensively. There, on the ledge, only Sniffles' tail is visible; the rest of him is hidden in the darkness of a foot-wide opening in the canyon wall. They will certainly be late getting back now, Marta thinks anxiously.

As Marta edges cautiously along the narrow ledge to grab her dog, Sniffles slips deeper inside the shadowy cave. Moments later, a shrill yelp pierces the air, and a furry flash bolts out of the cave. The dog sends Marta stumbling back, and she falls to the ground, sending pebbles clattering over the ledge into the deep canyon below. Frightened by her close call, Marta struggles to get to her feet just as a gray cloud of bats bursts from the cave. "Sniffles! Wait for me!" she cries, scrambling and sliding down the rocky slope behind her dog.

The startled explorers kick up dust all the way down the canyon trail and they never look back, not once.

Marta will remember the cave later, when she encounters a threat more dangerous than the desert and closer than she ever imagined.

2

3

Canyon Mystery

Fiction level U
Total words: 580
Average sentence length: 12.3 words

This text is the first chapter of a longer story, inviting the reader to predict the events that will follow, events that are foreshadowed by the girl's father's urgent admonition to return early, no matter what. Marta and her dog Sniffles are exploring a valley in New Mexico. Marta loves the beauty of the mesa. Suddenly Sniffles barks and runs away. They discover a cave with bats. The chapter ends with the idea that Marta will remember the cave later when she encounters a threat more dangerous than the desert.

Text characteristics:

▶ parallel between the danger in the desert and the implied threat communicated by Marta's father

▶ present-tense, third-person narrative

▶ varied sentence length but many more than twenty words

▶ some distortion of words in print for dramatic effect ("*Where aaaare you?*")

▶ requires reader to envision the setting in order to understand danger

▶ requires reader to connect first paragraph with the last in order to predict what may come in the subsequent chapters

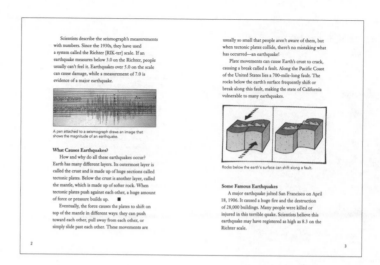

Earthquakes

Nonfiction level U
Total words: 489
Average sentence length: 15.0 words

This text begins with information about the destructive power of earthquakes and communicates the important idea that earthquakes occur across the planet every day, but the majority of them are so slight that people don't even know they are happening. The next three sections describe how to measure earthquakes, the causes of earthquakes, and some famous earthquakes. An important idea in the final section is that earthquakes are so dangerous because they cannot be clearly predicted.

Text characteristics:

▶ information presented with an introduction and four sections with headings

▶ requires inference that the tectonic plates are constantly moving

▶ requires understanding of historical information

▶ some technical vocabulary (*fault, Richter scale, seismologists, tectonic plates, tremors*)

▶ pronunciation guide in parentheses for technical words

▶ photographs with captions

▶ diagrams illustrating the shifting along a fault

▶ chart detailing famous earthquakes

▶ glossary

A Call for Change
by Sarah Wolbach

In this essay, Rachel writes to the editor of the newspaper to make a proposal. Read to find out the problem she wants to solve.

Fountas and Pinnell Benchmark Assessment System 2

Obviously, I hope that our mayor and city council members will see merit in my ideas and take action to implement them.

My concern is the lack of facilities available for young people like me to stay safely occupied and productive during the hours we are not in school. It is a fact that young people in Charlottesville spend only 20% of their time in school—six hours a day, 180 days per year. What they do with the other 80% is one of the most significant questions facing our community. ■

Kids are hanging out downtown, with nothing to do and nowhere to go. Business owners don't want kids like me in their shops. They say that shoplifting is a problem and that groups of unruly kids scare off their other customers. Police officers don't want kids loitering idly on the streets or in the city square. Consider this: Would we be hanging around bothering people if we had something better to do? It's not likely.

My suggestion is to rehabilitate the old Plainview Middle School, which has been closed for years, and open a community center to offer social, recreational, and educational activities for kids. If adults want kids to spend their time productively, they should be willing to offer rich and challenging activities to help us learn, explore

our talents, and develop positive relationships with peers and adults. And the center can offer opportunities for adults, too. That way, everybody wins!

And while we're on the subject, I wouldn't be surprised if plenty of those "unruly" kids wanted to serve their community right now. I would like to see the mayor set up a youth board. This group of committed teens could identify youth issues within the city. The board would then work together with the mayor and city and state officials to identify resources, develop solutions, and make improvements.

I know some people will say that this city has budget problems, and that there's not even enough money to repair the potholes in the streets. But here is my question: Can this city afford not to do this? It's true that it will cost money to pay for the services I propose. Many adults are just flat against raising taxes. To them I say this: We are your neighbors. We are part of this community that we all share. The problem I described belongs to all of us, because all of us care about the kind of city we live in. The future of your youth is in your hands. Do the right thing! Give me and other kids the programs we need to stay safe, learn, and grow into successful adults that everyone can be proud of.

2   3

A Call for Change

Fiction level V
Total words: 479
Average sentence length: 15.6 words

This fictional text presents a persuasive essay calling for a change in a community. The challenge in this text is that the genre appears to be informational (essay) even though it is fictional. At the beginning, a brief introduction sets the scene by providing the information that Rachel is the winner of an eighth-grade essay contest. It foreshadows the idea that Rachel has a forceful personality. The essay outlines a problem—that kids are hanging around downtown with nothing to do. It also makes a concrete proposal—to rehabilitate the old middle school and open a community center to provide educational and recreational opportunities for kids.

Text characteristics:

▶ persuasive essay—nonfiction format although fictional

▶ requires inference to understand Rachel's personality

▶ requires understanding of the problem and the specific proposal by Rachel to solve it

▶ parenthetical material set off by dashes in the middle of sentences

▶ many multisyllabic words, including some with five syllables

▶ requires understanding of the art of persuasion and ability to find examples in the text

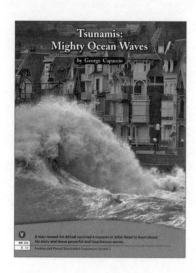

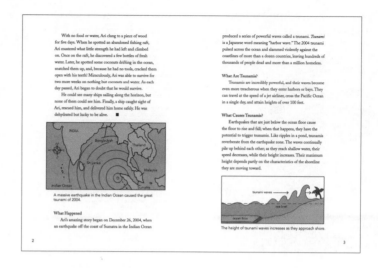

Tsunamis: Mighty Ocean Waves

Nonfiction level V
Total words: 503
Average sentence length: 16.8 words

This text begins with the story of Ari Afrizal, an Indonesian man who survived for almost three weeks in the ocean during the 2004 tsunami. This dramatic tale is followed by four sections describing this specific tsunami and then defining and explaining the causes of the giant waves. The book ends with a short section explaining that the only way for people to protect themselves from tsunamis is to head for higher ground.

Text characteristics:

▶ presents information in four sections with headings

▶ begins with a real story, adding drama to the text

▶ varied sentence length with some more than twenty-five words

▶ some technical vocabulary (*tsunami, aftershock, reverberate*)

▶ smaller font than previous levels

▶ photographs with captions

▶ maps and drawings with labels

▶ chart detailing dates and deadly tsunamis

▶ glossary

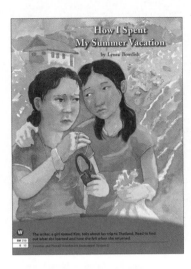

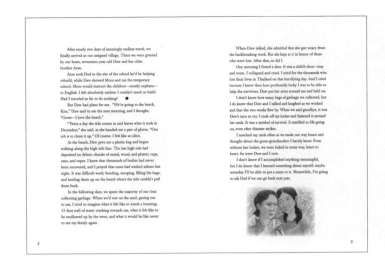

How I Spent My Summer Vacation

Fiction level W
Total words: 659
Average sentence length: 13.6 words

This story, told in first person as if in a diary entry, describes Lynea's experience volunteering in Thailand to help with disaster relief after the 2004 tsunami. Initially, Lynea doesn't want to go, but having no other option, she accompanies her parents on the trip. She wears the locket that her great-grandmother gave her—the only thing that was saved when an earthquake devastated her family's *pension* in Italy many years ago. This locket comes to be a symbol of survival as Lynea learns more about the human disaster and about herself.

Text characteristics:

- ▶ begins with a date as in a diary entry

- ▶ first-person narrative

- ▶ character development in that Lynea changes as she realizes the gravity of the situation

- ▶ turning point when Lynea finds the student's shoe and breaks down and cries for the thousands who lost their lives

- ▶ use of the locket as a symbol of survival

- ▶ sophisticated subject matter

- ▶ visual images of the crashing of thirty-three-foot walls of water

- ▶ many sentences with fifteen to twenty or more words

- ▶ mostly familiar vocabulary

Obituary: Coretta Scott King 1927–2006

Nonfiction level W
Total words: 575
Average sentence length: 19.8 words

The genre of this text is a newspaper article, an obituary of Coretta Scott King. It contains information about Coretta's birth, life, and death, including her role as wife of Dr. Martin Luther King. One of the main ideas of the article is that Coretta not only supported her husband's causes but continued his work after his death. The article includes quotes about Mrs. King, including comments on her never-ending fight for equality.

Text characteristics:

▶ begins with date and summary of King's life and death

▶ inset quote from Coretta Scott King

▶ information presented in three sections with headings

▶ requires understanding of the format of an obituary

▶ requires understanding of the setting

▶ words to be understood in context (*discrimination, Civil Rights, assassinated, boycott*)

▶ varied sentence length with some sentences more than thirty words

▶ requires understanding of Coretta's continuation of the campaign for equality

▶ photo with caption

▶ timeline

▶ glossary

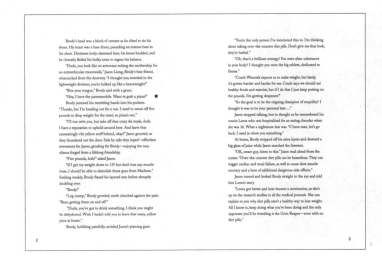

A Weighty Decision

Fiction level X
Total words: 682
Average sentence length: 11.8 words

In this story, Brody faces a significant decision—trying with all possible means to lose weight for the wrestling tournament or following his best friend's advice to take care of his health. He makes his decision based on his best friend Jason's account of his cousin Leora's eating disorder. The two boys also find information on the Internet that leads Brody to decide to protect his health.

Text characteristics:

- ▶ requires reader to recognize internal conflict in a character

- ▶ requires inference to recognize main character's motivations

- ▶ requires close attention to detail to learn that the main character is only thinking of taking diet pills, not actually taking them

- ▶ colloquial dialogue between teen characters

- ▶ extensive use of figurative language (*opponent* as a mound of clothing; head as *block of cement*; *wrestling with the Grim Reaper*)

- ▶ some very difficult vocabulary (*leviathan, nauseatingly, concoction, nutritionist*) but no technical words

- ▶ many long sentences, some with more than thirty words

- ▶ full range of punctuation including dashes and ellipses

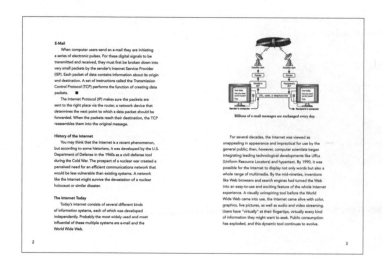

The Internet: Getting Connected

Nonfiction level X
Total words: 643
Average sentence length: 20.1 words

This text explains how the Internet works and provides information about its interesting history. For example, the Internet has been around since the 1960s when (according to some historians) it was created by the U.S. Department of Defense as a civil defense tool. Information is presented in five sections with headings. The Internet is defined and described, along with explanations as to why it has become so popular recently.

Text characteristics

- ▶ requires understanding of historical information; for example, *civil defense*, *Cold War*

- ▶ some information in chronological order

- ▶ requires readers to predict uses of the Internet

- ▶ long sentences, many more than thirty words

- ▶ many longer multisyllabic words

- ▶ includes technical vocabulary (*protocol*, *electronic pulses*, *digital*, *data packet*, *hypertext*)

- ▶ the word *virtually* used with two different definitions for a play on words

- ▶ pie graph with key

- ▶ diagram with labels to show how e-mail works

- ▶ drawing with legend to show hypertext

- ▶ glossary

Saying Goodbye

Fiction level Y
Total words: 711
Average sentence length: 13.6

This story, told in first-person narrative, begins with the central character talking directly to his friend Gerald, who died in an accident six months earlier. It then flashes back to the time of the accident and then forward to the present. Luis depended on Gerald, who always reassured and encouraged him. Gradually, Luis realizes that he needs to move on with his life, although he will always remember his friend.

Text characteristics:

▶ first-person narrative

▶ changes from present tense to past and back to present

▶ uses flashback

▶ turning point on page 3 with e-mail from Celine

▶ changes audience—from addressing Gerald to addressing the reader

▶ mature content

▶ varied sentence length with most fifteen to twenty-five words

▶ includes figurative language (*death slashes into our lives like a blade slashes skin*)

▶ many multisyllabic and/or difficult words (*prescient, philosophical, perspective*)

▶ some Spanish words

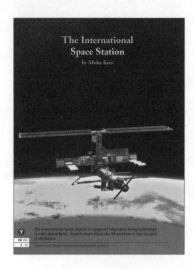

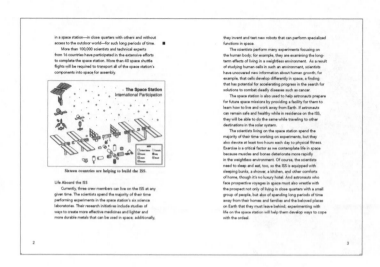

The International Space Station

Nonfiction level Y
Total words: 653
Average sentence length: 27.8 words

This book describes the International Space Station (ISS) that is now being assembled in orbit. The information is presented in three sections with headings. First, the station is described, along with its purposes. Then, life aboard the ISS is described, including what it is like to live in space and the kinds of experiments scientists can do there. Some significant issues are presented—the problems related to living in close quarters with a small group of people and leaving families for a long period of time. The last section presents problems to be solved.

Text characteristics:

▶ informational text presented in three sections with headings

▶ many long sentences, most fifteen to twenty-five words

▶ some technical words and many difficult multisyllabic words (*gravity, environmental, adaptations, psychologically, contemplating, initiatives, prospective*)

▶ use of acronyms

▶ photograph with caption

▶ diagram with legend

▶ glossary

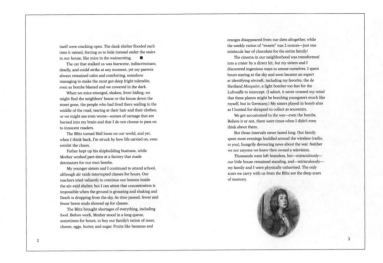

Surviving the Blitz

Fiction level Z
Total words: 639
Average sentence length: 21.6 words

This fictional text is written as a memoir. Told in first-person narrative, past tense turning to present at the end, the memories of Margaret Davies are recounted. She was only 11 years old in 1940 when the Blitz began and bombs fell for 57 days. Margaret describes the experience, using the metaphor of a cat to represent the lightning war and that of mice hiding in the wainscoting to represent the terrified Londoners. Readers will infer two important ideas: that people get used even to this kind of experience and try to go on with their daily lives as if it is normal; and even though Margaret and her family were not physically harmed, they will always carry the scars of terror.

Text characteristics:

- ▸ written as a memoir, although fictional
- ▸ knowledge of historical content required
- ▸ begins with a question and answer that sum up the content
- ▸ many long sentences, some forty or more words
- ▸ descriptive language
- ▸ many sophisticated words (*pulverizing, indiscriminate, tolerable, valiantly, concentration, queue, wireless*)
- ▸ figurative language (*the cat that stalked us, deep scars of memory*)
- ▸ German and French words in italics

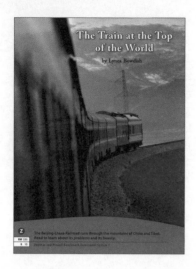

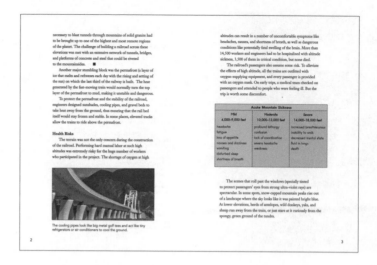

The Train at the Top of the World

Nonfiction level Z
Total words: 639
Average sentence length: 23.4 words

This text provides information about the Beijing-Lhasa Railroad, the highest railroad in the world (between 13,123 and 16,640 feet above sea level). The railroad was extremely difficult to build and its life may be temporary since it is built on fragile permafrost. Passengers see unbelievable vistas from the train but at the same time must be protected by special tinted windows (to protect them from ultraviolet rays) and often must be given oxygen. The railroad opens trade between two regions that were difficult to access prior to its construction. Information is presented in three sections with headings.

Text characteristics:

▶ text presented in three sections with headings

▶ many long sentences, some more than forty words

▶ many difficult multisyllable words (*permafrost, riveted, ultraviolet, unprecedented, terrain, potentially*)

▶ map with key

▶ photographs with captions

▶ chart providing information about mountain sickness

▶ glossary

Appendix B: Assessment Forms Book and CD-ROM

All record-keeping forms for the Fountas & Pinnell Benchmark Assessment System are available in the *Assessment Forms* book as well as in electronic form on the *Assessment Forms* CD-ROM. The following tools are found in both.

Assessment Forms

Recording Forms

The Recording Form is the primary tool for administering the Benchmark Assessment. With it, you observe and code the reader's oral reading behaviors, comprehension conversation, and (optionally) Writing About Reading. There are thirty Recording Forms in *Fountas & Pinnell Benchmark Assessment System 2*, one for each benchmark book.

Summary Forms

1 The Assessment Summary form organizes and displays assessment results from multiple Recording Forms on multiple book readings. The final benchmark levels—Independent, Instructional, and Recommended Placement—as well as additional observations and instructional implications are recorded here.

2 The Bi-annual, Tri-annual, and Quarterly Assessment Summary forms provide three options for tracking student progress across a school year. Choose the one that reflects the number of times in a school year you plan to administer Benchmark Assessments: two (bi-annual), three (tri-annual), or four (quarterly). On this form you record the information from the Assessment Summary form for the Benchmark Independent and Instructional levels.

3 The Class Record form provides a way for you to see all your students' assessment data in relation to each other. It combines the Benchmark Independent- and Instructional-level information; the accuracy, comprehension, and fluency scores; and Recommended Placement level for each student onto a class list and is useful for determining groups and differentiating instruction.

4 Two Records of Reading Progress give you a picture of progress through the benchmark levels. The Annual Record of Reading Progress is designed for teacher use across one school year. In addition to charting the results of Benchmark Assessments, it may also include interim levels from ongoing running records. The Longitudinal Record of Reading Progress is printed on the student folder as well as in the *Assessment Forms* book and CD-ROM. This progress form can be passed from teacher to teacher over the years of schooling from grade K to middle school to show progress over time.

Optional Assessments

Where-to-Start Word Test

The Where-to-Start Word Test provides a quick way to quickly find a starting place for the text reading assessment. If you do not have sufficient information from the previous teacher or school records or your own observations to judge the starting point for the assessment, this test should save you from having the student read a large number of texts. The Where-to-Start Word Test is a series of lists of increasingly difficult words, organized by grade level. The student's level of performance reading the words predicts the approximate level of text that the student may be able to read.

Reading Interview

The Reading Interview is an optional form that you can use to learn more about a reader's preferences and reading history. It takes about five minutes to administer the interview.

Six Dimensions Fluency Rubric

The Six Dimensions Fluency Rubric provides a detailed way to look at oral reading fluency. It targets five dimensions of fluency—pausing, phrasing, stress, intonation, and rate—and a sixth dimension, integration, which refers to the way the reader orchestrates the other five dimensions. The scale can be used to provide more in-depth evaluation than the simple fluency score on the Fountas & Pinnell Benchmark Assessment System. It can also be used whenever you are observing a reader's behavior, not just during benchmark testing, to assess the aspects of fluency that the reader is demonstrating and those neglected. You can then plan and shape your teaching to do some very specific demonstration and prompting for various aspects of fluency.

Phonics and Word Analysis Assessments

Phonics and Word Analysis Assessments focus on specific reading-processing skills: high frequency words, phonograms, blends, clusters, suffixes, prefixes, and multisyllabic words. Your school or district may want to select an optional assessment that you feel is critical for a particular grade level as part of the Benchmark Assessment process. Or you may want to diagnose a particular area of learning (such as reading words with vowel clusters) for a student who shows difficulty. If most of your class or a small group is having difficulty in an area (for example, reading two-syllable words), you might want to give them the assessment. In any case, select only assessments that are needed for a particular purpose.

Phonics and Word Analysis Assessments

	Assessment	Category of Learning	Description
1	Reading High Frequency Words: 100 words	High frequency words	Students read 100 high frequency words.
2	Reading High Frequency Words: 200 words	High frequency words	Students read 200 high frequency words.
3	Phonograms I	Spelling patterns	Students read words with simple phonogram patterns.
4	Phonograms II	Spelling patterns	Students read words with more difficult phonogram patterns.
5	Consonant Blends	Letter-sound relationships	Students say words and identify consonant clusters.
6	Vowel Clusters	Letter-sound relationships	Students read words with vowels that appear together and represent one sound.
7	Suffixes I	Word structure	Students read words with suffixes that change the part of speech.
8	Suffixes II	Word structure	Students read words with more difficult suffixes.
9	Prefixes	Word structure	Students read words with prefixes.
10	Compound Words	Word structure	Students read simple compound words and identify the two words that have been put together.
11	One- and Two-Syllable Words	Word structure	Students say a word, clap or tap a finger for each syllable, and then identify the number of syllables in the word.
12	Syllables in Longer Words	Word structure	Students demonstrate that they understand the concept of syllables, can hear syllable breaks, can count the number of syllables in a word, and have a beginning understanding of where to divide a word when hyphenating.

Optional Phonics and Word Analysis Assessments

Continued on next page

	Assessment	Category of Learning	Description
Phonics and Word Analysis Assessments			
13	Grade 2 Word Features Test	Letter-sound recognition	Students read 30 words, which include a variety of features: possessives, double vowels, multisyllabic words, long vowel sounds, contractions, *y* as a vowel sound, prefixes, consonant clusters, consonant digraphs, double vowels.
14	Grade 3 Word Features Test	Word structure	Students read 30 words, which include a variety of features: phonogram patterns in monosyllabic words, syllable patterns in multisyllabic words, consonant digraphs, contractions, prefixes, compound words.
15	Grade 4 Word Features Test	Word structure	Students read 30 words, which include a variety of features: double consonants, syllable patterns in multisyllabic words, phonogram patterns in monosyllabic words, contractions, consonant digraphs, prefixes.
16	Grade 5 Word Features Test	Word structure	Students read 30 words, which include a variety of features: vowel patterns in multisyllabic words, double consonants, word endings, plural possessives, prefixes.
17	Grade 6 Word Features Test	Word structure	Students read 30 words, which include a variety of features: word endings, plural possessives, prefixes, Greek or Latin roots.
18	Grade 7–8 Word Features Test	Word structure	Students read 30 words, which include a variety of features: word endings, plural possessives, prefixes, Greek or Latin roots, taking apart multisyllabic words.

Optional Phonics and Word Analysis Assessments

Vocabulary Assessments

A selection of Vocabulary Assessments focuses on word meaning and evaluates a student's word knowledge (concept words, vocabulary in context), understanding of word relationships (synonyms, antonyms, roots, analogies), and ability to derive the precise meaning of words in the context of a short book (vocabulary in context).

	Name	Category	Description
	Vocabulary Assessments		
	Name	**Category**	**Description**
1	Concept Words	Vocabulary	Students read concept words and sort them into appropriate categories.
2	Synonyms I	Vocabulary	Students read and identify words that mean the same or almost the same.
3	Synonyms II	Vocabulary	Students identify words that mean the same or almost the same.
4	Antonyms I	Vocabulary	Students read and identify words that mean the opposite or almost the opposite.
5	Antonyms II	Vocabulary	Students identify words that mean the opposite or almost the opposite.
6	Homophones I	Vocabulary	Students read a sentence with a blank space and choose the correct homophone from two or three words.
7	Homophones II	Vocabulary	Students read a sentence with a blank space and choose the correct homophone from two or three words.
8	Homographs	Vocabulary	Students read aloud sentence pairs that have homographs.
9	Greek and Latin Word Roots	Vocabulary	Students correctly identify the meaning of Greek and Latin roots by looking at a list of words that include each root.
10	Analogies	Vocabulary	Students identify the relationship between two words and choose another pair of words that exhibits the same relationship.
11	Level L fiction	Vocabulary in context	Students use context to correctly identify the meaning of five words from the book *Ernie Learns*.
12	Level L nonfiction	Vocabulary in context	Students use context to correctly identify the meaning of five words from the book *Hang On, Baby Monkey*.

Vocabulary Assessments

Continued on next page

Vocabulary Assessments

	Name	Category	Description
13	Level M fiction	Vocabulary in context	Students use context to correctly identify the meaning of five words from the book *Saving Up*.
14	Level M nonfiction	Vocabulary in context	Students use context to correctly identify the meaning of five words from the book *City Hawks*.
15	Level N fiction	Vocabulary in context	Students use context to correctly identify the meaning of five words from the book *Vanessa's Butterfly*.
16	Level N nonfiction	Vocabulary in context	Students use context to correctly identify the meaning of five words from the book *Dogs at Work*.
17	Level O fiction	Vocabulary in context	Students use context to correctly identify the meaning of five words from the book *The New Girl*.
18	Level O nonfiction	Vocabulary in context	Students use context to correctly identify the meaning of five words from the book *Snake Myths*.
19	Level P fiction	Vocabulary in context	Students use context to correctly identify the meaning of five words from the book *Plenty of Pets*.
20	Level P nonfiction	Vocabulary in context	Students use context to correctly identify the meaning of five words from the book *Animal Instincts*.
21	Level Q fiction	Vocabulary in context	Students use context to correctly identify the meaning of five words from the book *A Secret Home*.
22	Level Q nonfiction	Vocabulary in context	Students use context to correctly identify the meaning of five words from the book *Not Too Cold for a Polar Bear*.
23	Level R fiction	Vocabulary in context	Students use context to correctly identify the meaning of five words from the book *The Election*.
24	Level R nonfiction	Vocabulary in context	Students use context to correctly identify the meaning of five words from the book *Fishing Smarts*.
25	Level S fiction	Vocabulary in context	Students use context to correctly identify the meaning of five words from the book *Could Be Worse*.
26	Level S nonfiction	Vocabulary in context	Students use context to correctly identify the meaning of five words from the book *Amazing Animal Adaptations*.
27	Level T fiction	Vocabulary in context	Students use context to correctly identify the meaning of five words from the book *"Get a Horse!"*
28	Level T nonfiction	Vocabulary in context	Students use context to correctly identify the meaning of five words from the book *Why Do Wolves Howl?*

Vocabulary Assessments

Continued on next page

Fountas & Pinnell Benchmark 2 Assessment Guide

	Name	Category	Description
Vocabulary Assessments			
29	Level U fiction	Vocabulary in context	Students use context to correctly identify the meaning of five words from the book *Canyon Mystery*.
30	Level U nonfiction	Vocabulary in context	Students use context to correctly identify the meaning of five words from the book *Earthquakes*.
31	Level V fiction	Vocabulary in context	Students use context to correctly identify the meaning of five words from the book *A Call for Change*.
32	Level V nonfiction	Vocabulary in context	Students use context to correctly identify the meaning of five words from the book *Tsunamis: Mighty Ocean Waves*.
33	Level W fiction	Vocabulary in context	Students use context to correctly identify the meaning of five words from the book *How I Spent My Summer Vacation*.
34	Level W nonfiction	Vocabulary in context	Students use context to correctly identify the meaning of five words from the book *Obituary: Coretta Scott King*.
35	Level X fiction	Vocabulary in context	Students use context to correctly identify the meaning of five words from the book *A Weighty Decision*.
36	Level X nonfiction	Vocabulary in context	Students use context to correctly identify the meaning of five words from the book *The Internet: Getting Connected*.
37	Level Y fiction	Vocabulary in context	Students use context to correctly identify the meaning of five words from the book *Saying Goodbye*.
38	Level Y nonfiction	Vocabulary in context	Students use context to correctly identify the meaning of five words from the book *The International Space Station*.
39	Level Z fiction	Vocabulary in context	Students use context to correctly identify the meaning of five words from the book *Surviving the Blitz*.
40	Level Z nonfiction	Vocabulary in context	Students use context to correctly identify the meaning of five words from the book *Train at the Top of the World*.

Vocabulary Assessments

Resources

Each of these charts summarizes a key Benchmark Assessment procedure.

▶ **Assessment at-a-Glance** provides a reference for the assessment conference.

▶ **Coding and Scoring Errors at-a-Glance** describes the coding and scoring of errors and self-corrections in an oral reading evaluation.

▶ **Guide for Observing and Noting Reading Behaviors** lists questions to help you analyze the ways a reader is processing text.

▶ **Scoring and Analysis at-a-Glance** summarizes how to make the final calculations and observations.

▶ The **Text Gradient** correlates Fountas and Pinnell levels with grade levels.

▶ **Finding Easy, Instructional, and Hard Texts** is a quick reference for selecting the right benchmark books during an assessment conference.

Assessment Forms Book and CD-ROM

All of the assessment forms are available either in reproducible form in the *Assessment Forms* book or as printable PDF files on the *Assessment Forms* CD-ROM. On the CD-ROM, you can navigate to different tabs for Recording Forms, Summary Forms, Optional Assessments, and Resources. Then you can select which forms you want, view the files in Adobe Acrobat Reader, and print them as you wish.

You can select, view, and print Recording Forms by level, title, or genre. You can also print them with enlarged book text for easier reading and coding. Summary forms for a single assessment conference and forms for tracking a student's progress are also readily accessible.

The three parts of the optional assessments can be viewed and printed from the CD-ROM, either separately or together. To help you make decisions about which optional assessments to administer, you can also view and print the entire list to use as a reference.

The fourth tab offers the following resources:

▶ Assessment at-a-Glance

▶ Coding Errors

▶ Coding and Scoring at-a-Glance

▶ Scoring and Analysis at-a-Glance

▶ Guide for Observing and Noting Reading Behaviors

▶ Text Gradient

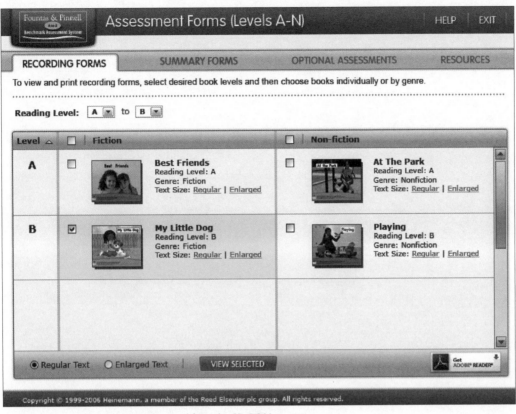

Recording Forms can be viewed and printed from the CD-ROM.

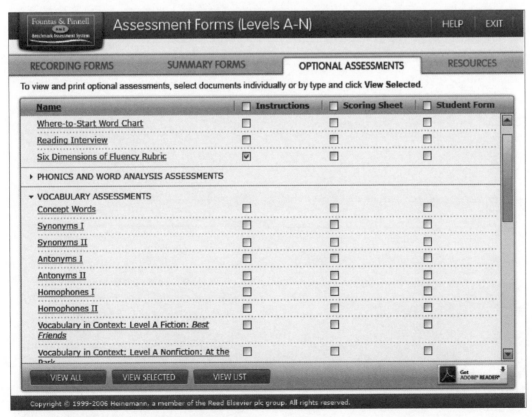

Select, view, and print any number of optional assessments.

Appendix C:
Data Management CD-ROM

The *Data Management* CD-ROM allows you to track and analyze assessment data for individual students and entire classes. Once you have logged in, you can create a class and enter student data, either manually or by importing it from another file.

After administering the assessments, you can enter assessment data from individual recording forms and/or the assessment summary forms. You can view an individual student's assessment summary for any administration period.

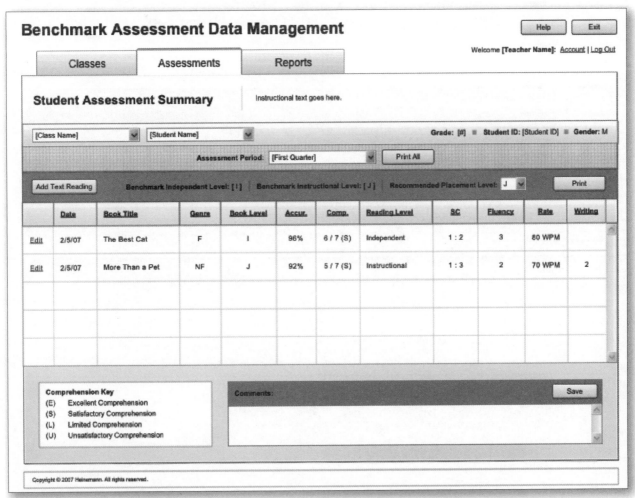

Individual student assessment summary

You can view a class assessment summary, including all students' benchmark levels and associated data. Class assessment summaries can also be printed by assessment administration period. To facilitate data analysis, records can be sorted by any data category. For example, to help you form instructional groups, student records can be sorted by Benchmark Instructional level.

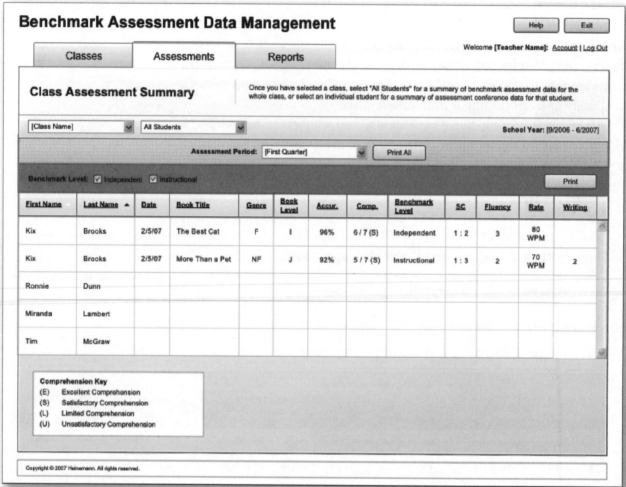

Class assessment summary

A variety of graphing options allow you to analyze assessment data to identify patterns and track progress over time. For example, you can create a report that graphs an individual student's Benchmark Instructional reading levels at several points in the school year.

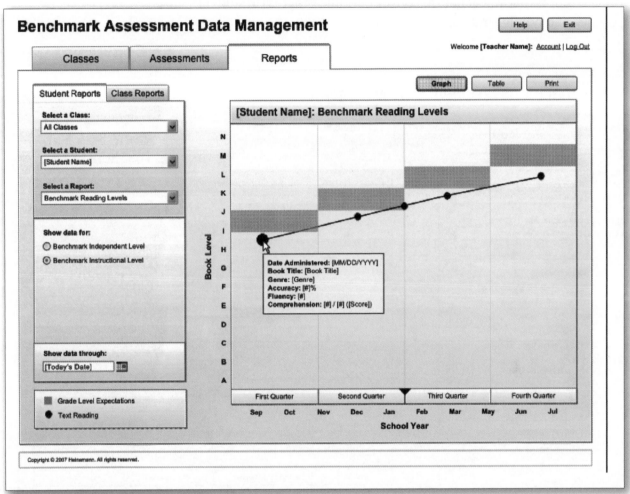

Individual student progress report showing benchmark levels for the school year

You can also graph benchmark levels or comprehension scores for an entire class to get a picture of overall performance. In order to inform instruction, teachers can use reports to reflect on student data patterns. For example, if your class reports show that students generally have high scores for "within the text" comprehension, but low scores for "beyond the text" comprehension, you might plan to focus subsequent instruction on making inferences and other interpretive skills. Printed reports allow teachers to convey periodic progress to students, parents, and administrators.

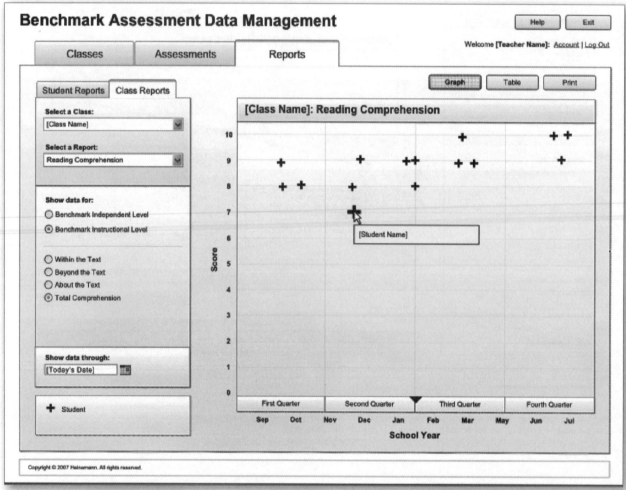

Class progress report indicating total comprehension scores for an entire class

Appendix D
Professional Development DVD

The *Professional Development* DVD allows teachers to view a variety of assessments in action. Its modular design offers teachers the opportunity to learn about each component of the benchmark assessment with varying degrees of guidance, depending on individual needs.

The *Professional Development* DVD provides the following options for learning about the Fountas and Pinnell Benchmark Assessment System:

- ▶ a general overview of the benchmark assessment system and its components

- ▶ explanations of each step in the benchmark assessment procedure, including preparation, book selection, oral readings, comprehension conversations, and optional student writing, as well as coding, scoring, analyzing, and interpreting an assessment

- ▶ guided tutorials that offer practice in coding oral reading behaviors

- ▶ instruction about scoring and analyzing oral reading behaviors, fluency, and comprehension, with authentic examples of student readings and comprehension conversations for demonstration and practice

- ▶ teacher reflections on benchmark assessments, considering their instructional implications for particular students

- ▶ a chance to practice applying new knowledge and skills while viewing a sample assessment conference from beginning to end

Kulsum reads *Bubbles* while Stephanie assesses her.

Frequently Asked Questions

General

What does the term *level* mean?

A level refers to the difficulty of the book in relation to other books placed along a continuum from A to Z, easiest to hardest. We examine the characteristics of a book and place it along a gradient of books in relation to each other. A level designates the books as easier than the level after (later in the alphabet) and harder than the level before it (earlier in the alphabet). We use ten characteristics to determine a level and the composite of characteristics contributes to its final designation. For a detailed explanation of each level, see *Leveled Books, K–8: Matching Texts to Readers for Effective Teaching* (Heinemann, 2006).

Do the Fountas & Pinnell Benchmark levels match the guided reading levels?

Yes. This assessment is specifically designed to match the guided reading levels described in *Leveled Books, K–8: Matching Texts to Readers for Effective Teaching* (Heinemann, 2006) and other publications by Fountas and Pinnell.

How can I use this benchmark system to match books leveled with other systems?

The website fountasandpinnellleveledbooks.com lists over 20,000 books leveled using the Fountas and Pinnell system, and the site is updated every month. Also, many publishers place several different kinds of levels on books and/or offer correlation charts. But you can also use the benchmark texts as models or prototypes to help you level other books. Then you can test your leveled books with students. Remember that in Benchmark 2, the texts are necessarily shorter than most of the texts students read.

Should I assess both fiction and nonfiction reading?

The fiction and nonfiction book at each level are equivalent measures. You can use either text to determine the child's ability to read at that level.

How long does it take to administer the assessment to a student?

At the earliest levels it may take fifteen or twenty minutes while it may take about thirty or forty minutes when your students are reading the longer texts and the discussions are more substantive. In this guide we make several suggestions on how to be efficient with your use of time.

How often should you administer the Benchmark Assessment?

We suggest that you administer the assessment at the beginning of the year to know where to start the teaching with each student. You may want to conduct the assessment in the middle of the year to take stock of student progress, though you may already have the information from your ongoing use of running records or reading records in instruction. At the end of the year you may want to make a final record of the student's growth across the year.

Are Benchmark Assessment books ones the students may have read before?

In the Benchmark Assessment the students are reading an unseen text, or a text that the student has not read before. You can expect the text to be a little harder than it would be if they have read it once before.

Is the Fountas & Pinnell Benchmark Assessment System a standardized test?

Yes, it is a standardized assessment. The administration, coding, scoring, and interpretation are standardized in procedures to get reliable results. We expect that once you get the standardized results, you will review the data to make good judgments for instruction. Good teacher decisions based on data are essential.

Is Benchmark Assessment authentic assessment?

You cannot get closer to authentic assessment than with the Fountas & Pinnell Benchmark Assessment System. The student reads several books, thinks and talks about them, and writes about reading. This is not only a valid assessment of the competencies you want to measure, but is a good use of teacher and student time!

Some teachers feel that the assessment is an accountability measure for them. Do you agree?

As teachers, we need to seek information about our students as well as information that informs us about how our teaching is impacting their learning. At the beginning of the year, the assessment gives information about the starting points of the learners. As the school year progresses, the assessment becomes a tool for measuring the growth of the students and the effectiveness of your teaching. The series of assessments conducted over several years will reflect the success of the entire school in bringing each child forward in literacy outcomes.

How does this Benchmark Assessment package help me with my leveled book program?

The Fountas & Pinnell Benchmark Assessment is designed to help you collect reliable evidence of student competencies and reading levels so you can begin your teaching where the learners are—at the optimal instructional level and with in-depth knowledge of his reading behaviors—bringing each reader forward in his competencies. No other assessment has been directly linked to the Fountas and Pinnell levels to date, so you will also have a reliable and valid assessment to link to guided reading small-group reading instruction.

How does the Benchmark Assessment support my ability to conduct the assessment conference with students whose first language is not English?

You will notice that in the Assessment Guide we have provided specific support to help you understand how language differences should be noticed in the administration and interpretation of the assessment. In addition, case examples of English language learners describe and comment on real situations for you to think about and learn from.

How does the Fountas and Pinnell Benchmark Assessment contribute to my knowledge of students and how they develop as readers?

You will find that the comprehensive assessment procedures and the variety of tools and options provided in the Benchmark Assessment package are rich resources for helping you systematically examine a student's strengths and needs and begin to think about the important link between assessment and instruction. You will find detailed information about analyzing the reading behaviors of the student and linking them to specific instructional goals in the Assessment Guide. The Guide for Observing and

Noting Reading Behaviors in the *Assessment Forms* book and CD-ROM is a learning tool in itself; it focuses attention on critical reading behaviors. *The Continuum of Literacy Learning: A Guide to Teaching* is the foundation for instruction; you will be able to make a direct link from the data gathered with the assessment to the continuum's specific behaviors to notice, teach, and support in every instructional context related to literacy. The *Professional Development* DVD is another rich resource; it is designed to help you conduct efficient and effective assessments, learn how to interpret the results, and connect your understandings to instruction. Over time, observations made through the assessment, instruction designed to move the student ahead from level to level, and follow-up assessment will deepen your understanding of literacy development.

How can the Fountas and Pinnell Benchmark Assessment System help upper-grade teachers learn about the reading process?

If you are an upper-grade teacher, you will find that Benchmark Assessment is the perfect starting point for learning to observe and code the reading behaviors of your students. The procedures supported by the Assessment Forms and the analysis training in the Assessment Guide and on the *Professional Development* DVD will help you observe and talk about your students' effective and ineffective behaviors and how the texts they are reading may be appropriate or inappropriate for supporting new learning. After a few months' experience with Benchmark Assessment conferences, you will become much more knowledgeable and interested in what your students are learning about the reading process and become increasingly effective at differentiating instruction.

Is there a place we can pose questions and get a response?

You can post your questions at www.fountas andpinnellbenchmarkassessment.com.

Administering the Assessment

How do you know at which level to start Benchmark Assessment so as to make the administration as time efficient as possible?

We provide several time-saving options. If you have no information on the student's previous reading, the Where-to-Start Word Test provides a rough starting level for assessment and will cut down the number of books a student needs to read before you can identify an independent and an instructional level. If you do have information about a student's previous reading performance, we provide several charts in the Assessment Guide that help determine the starting point by looking at the texts students are reading.

How can I ensure that I am conducting the assessment in a standardized manner?

The precise steps of the assessment conference are described in the Assessment Guide and systematically presented on the Recording Form for each book. The introduction is standardized and printed on the cover of the book as well as on the Recording Form. The steps of the administration, the scoring, and the analysis are all standardized. In addition, the tools supporting the assessment—the F & P Calculator/Stopwatch and the At-a-Glance charts (Assessment at-a-Glance and Coding and Scoring at-a-Glance)—provide an easy way to maintain consistency and help you internalize the steps. Further, the *Professional Development* DVD provides clear examples and plentiful practice opportunities for developing precision and consistency throughout assessment conferences.

Should I administer the assessment to a student who speaks very little English?

We suggest that you follow your school policy regarding the assessment of students whose first language is not English. If you would administer other standardized tests to those students, then you should administer this one. You will find that the gradient of texts will allow most children at least to begin to engage in the reading process.

Can I show the child the pictures during the introduction of the text?

Do not show the pictures during the introduction. The student may look at the front cover as you read the introduction. It is important to follow the standardized directions for the administration so your results will be consistent.

Why do we assess the child on a "cold" reading?

On a cold reading, with only a minimal introduction, you have the best opportunity to observe what the reader can do independently. It is important to have this information in order to guide the reader in his or her independent choices and to determine what the reader needs to learn next.

Why is the introduction so short? Why can't I tell the child more about the text?

Because you want to learn what the child can do independently, it is important not to tell him too much about the text in advance of reading. The introduction is scripted so that the assessment can be as standardized as possible. This standardization is necessary so that we can interpret the results for a class or a school of students.

Oral Reading

Is it permissible for the child to point and read the text?

Instruct the child to point under the words at Levels A and B. After that you do not tell the child to point or not to point. If a child is pointing beyond level C, you may want to make a note of it, as it is likely interfering with fluent, phrased reading.

What if I can't keep up with the coding and I miss some of the student errors?

If you find you cannot keep up with the coding, ask the student to stop until you catch up. The more experienced you get in administering the assessment, the faster your coding will go.

If the student is reading a text that is very hard, is it necessary for him to finish the text so I can determine accuracy level?

No, you can stop the reading early. You will want to say, "This is a very tricky story. You can stop there." As a teacher, you have gathered the data you need and you can discontinue the testing. There is no need to have the student continue to read if the accuracy rate has gone well below 90% for Levels A–K or 95% for Levels L–Z.

When I am assessing and the first book the student reads is too hard, what should I do?

You should judge how hard the book is and move down at least a couple of levels so you can find the easy level and the instructional level.

When I am assessing a student, can I skip levels?

Of course you can skip levels. Your goal is to have the student read the fewest number of books that will give you the data you need as efficiently as possible. If you find a text is very easy, you may want to skip a level or more to get to one that is closer to instructional level. The same applies when a text is very hard and you need to find an instructional level; in this case you may want to skip down some levels.

The directions sometimes indicate the student should continue to read the text silently; wouldn't it be better if I listened to the student read the whole book?

No. It is important to give the student the opportunity to process the text without the oral reinforcement. The oral reading also slows the reader down.

At what level should I expect the student to read fluently?

You should expect the student to read with phrasing and fluency as soon as the early reading behaviors are well under control. We expect the behaviors to be well under control at about the end of Level B or beginning of Level C in instruction. Readers will not be reading fast with complete fluency at the early levels because they are still learning ways of processing print. You should expect, though, to see some phrasing, especially on texts that have dialogue.

Should the child who is reading Level A and B read fluently?

No, you want the child to slow down his language to read one word at a time. At these levels the child is learning to match one spoken word with one printed word. Slow, careful pointing and reading is what you are helping the child control.

Is fluency a stage of reading?

No. Fluency is not a stage of reading. After about level C, readers can read with phrasing and fluency at every level if it is within instructional or independent range.

Do I have to calculate the oral reading rate?

We recommend calculating reading rate only at levels J and above. We have provided you with a formula for calculating reading rate on the Recording Form. You may also use the F & P Calculator/Stopwatch provided with this assessment system to get a quick and accurate score.

Is rate an important factor when children are just beginning to learn to read?

We suggest that you begin to notice the reading rate at about the beginning of grade 2 as one indicator of fluency.

What is the appropriate oral reading rate for each level?

We have provided ranges for reading rate. See the table on page 39.

Why is reading rate important?

Reading rate is one indicator of whether the reader is putting groups of words together in processing the text. When a student is reading one word at a time, the reading gets bogged down and the student is not likely to be able to attend to the meaning of the text.

Comprehension Conversation

Can a child look back at the text during the comprehension conversation?

Though you should not instruct the student to do so, it is permissible for the child to initiate looking back in the text. If the student begins to read the text, ask him to tell the response in his own words.

What happens if the child has to refer back to the text to answer a question? Does this affect his comprehension score?

If a child initiates looking back in the text, locates the information, and provides a correct response, you should give credit for the answer.

Looking back in the text will not affect the comprehension score unless the child is simply pointing at or rereading some of the text to you. Then say, "Tell me in your own words."

What if the child does not understand the question?

Be sure to rephrase the question until the child understands it. Your goal is to determine whether the student understood the information in the story, not whether the student understood the question.

How can I keep up with the note taking?

After you have administered the conversation one or two times, you will be able to interpret the student's comments and connect them to the "key understandings" in the first column. Check the ones the student has covered and take notes only on the additional information provided by the student (if any). Also, you can take a quick moment to make these checks right after the conversation (while the student is writing or after she leaves).

What should I do if the student does not come up with the key understandings?

You can use the probes or questions to elicit answers. You do not need to score the student lower because you had to probe for answers. Some children are not accustomed to spontaneously talking about their thinking, yet they may understand the text very well and demonstrate it when questioned.

Should I "count" the "right answers" the student makes in order to come up with the comprehension score?

No. These texts vary and have different requirements in terms of key understandings (thinking within, beyond, and about the text). Look at the rubric for scoring each category (within, beyond, and about). Make a holistic decision as to the extent to which the student has demonstrated thinking.

Where can I find more information about thinking within, beyond, and about the text?

You will find very detailed descriptions in *Teaching for Comprehending and Fluency: Thinking, Talking, and Writing About Reading, K–8* by Fountas and Pinnell (Heinemann, 2006).

How can I make the comprehension conversation sound "natural"?

You will find some suggestions on page 29 of this guide.

Interpreting & Reporting Results

What if the student achieves instructional or independent level at two levels?

Occasionally you will find that a student performs the same on two levels of text. Use the *higher* of the levels as your indicator.

What if a student reads a text at the instructional level and then a higher level (harder) text at the independent level?

You will want to have the student try another more difficult text to see if the independent level was achieved because the topic was easy. If this text is hard for the student, you will probably want to begin at the original instructional level. If this text is easy for the student, continue until you find another instructional level and begin there. When you begin teaching, you will have the opportunity to observe the reader closely with other texts and can always move up or down a level and change groups if needed.

Does the student's guided reading group have to be at her instructional level?

No. The "Recommended Placement Level," which is the recommended level for guided reading, may be a level lower or higher, depending on your analysis. Pages 44 to 48 describe the thinking process involved in finding a placement level.

What if I have students on six or seven different placement levels? Should I have that many guided reading groups?

It is very difficult to have a large number of reading groups. It makes it hard for you to provide instruction to students on a regular basis because you certainly cannot see all groups every day or even over a week. As you look over your Recommended Placement Levels, you may have to put students who have different instructional levels in a single group. Try to vary your interactions within the group accordingly, giving some students more support and others more challenge (for example, with writing). Most teachers find it difficult to work with more than four or five groups.

What if I have a student who is so far ahead of the class that he doesn't belong in any group?

This kind of student can enjoy participating with the fastest progress group because he will benefit from discussion with others and there is always something more to learn. Advanced readers often read books that are easy for them. Remember that these groups are dynamic, so you can always invite the student to participate in reading some texts and not others. In addition, you will want to provide challenging independent reading for the student (extended through individual conferences).

What if I have a student who reads far above grade level (for example, a first grader who reads level O)?

Look carefully at the comprehension. Chances are, this student has literal comprehension, but lacks rich understanding. Another factor to consider is stamina. The student may be able to read and even have minimal understanding of a high level text; however, it may not be a good experience for her to plow through long chapter books on a regular basis. In general, students enjoy age-appropriate material, so you can extend this student by providing texts just one or two grade levels above her present one. There are always a few students who are truly exceptional, and for those readers you have to make individual decisions.

What if I have a student who reads at a level far below the rest of the students?

This student needs intervention to make accelerated progress, so the first thing to do is to try to get some extra services. At the same time, this student desperately needs classroom instruction, so you should try not to remove him from all of the teaching you are providing. If at all possible, provide enough individual support that the student can participate in a group and can make better progress.

What if I have a student who reads a level with accuracy and understanding but is not at all fluent? Should I go down a level for instruction?

You might want to go down a level, but that is not always the answer. Some students have developed a habit of reading dysfluently and might do so even at easy levels. You'll want to look in greater depth at the student's reading. We suggest using the Six Dimensions Fluency Rubric in the *Assessment Forms* book and CD-ROM so that you can decide with more precision what to teach the student. Sometimes, if accuracy and understanding are there, you can teach intensively for fluency and get a shift in a short time.

How will I know how assessment level relates to our standards for grade level performance in our district?

Your school and your district should make decisions about expected grade level standards, taking into account your state goals. You can refer to our Text Gradient chart (see page 2) for suggested indicators, but adjust them if you have rationales for a different standard.

How can we use the Benchmark Assessment data to improve our school?

Have regular faculty meetings to examine the data within and across grade levels. Look at the general reading levels of the age cohort, but don't stop there. Use the case examples in the guide to help you think about some priorities for teaching students. Think across the language and literacy framework. You can teach for comprehending through interactive read aloud, minilessons, guided reading, and literature discussion. Use *The Continuum of Literacy Learning: A Guide to Teaching* in the benchmark system to find teaching goals.

How can I pass information along to ensure that my students' literacy growth will be documented across the years?

You will find a variety of tools in the Benchmark Assessment package to support the documentation of a student's growth over time as well as ways to track development of whole groups. The *Assessment Forms* CD-ROM provides several options for reports on an individual or the whole class in report or graph format; the *Data Management* CD-ROM makes this even easier. The Student Folder also provides a longitudinal graph for teachers to record progress each year. The folder is designed to be passed from teacher to teacher, from one grade to the next, and to hold the assessment information on one student across nine years, from kindergarten to grade 8.

Is there a way for our school's Benchmark Assessment data to be linked to the district office?

Yes. Heinemann provides an option for districts to link school data to the central office data system.

Glossary

► **A**

Accuracy (as in oral reading) or **accuracy rate** The percentage of words the student reads aloud correctly

Analyzing a reading record Looking at errors, self-corrections, and sources of information to plan instruction

Annual Record of Reading Progress A graph showing a student's progress through reading levels across one grade or year; located in *Assessment Forms*

Appeal (in benchmark reading assessment) A reader's verbal or nonverbal request for help

Assessment at-a-Glance A chart containing a brief summary of the steps in administering the Benchmark Assessment (see inside front cover and *Assessment Forms*)

Assessment conference A one-on-one teacher-student Benchmark Assessment session

Assessment Summary The Benchmark Assessment form that combines the results of multiple benchmark book readings from the Recording Forms and guides identification of Benchmark Independent, Benchmark Instructional, and Recommended Placement levels; located in *Assessment Forms*

► **B**

Basal reading program A multigrade series, usually of textbook anthologies, with an established scope and sequence of skills

Benchmark Book The leveled text a student reads during Benchmark Assessment

Bi-annual Assessment Summary A form that compiles Assessment Summary results from assessment conferences conducted two times during a school year; located in *Assessment Forms*

► **C**

Class Record A chart containing a class list on which to record students' independent and/ or instructional levels in order to see a group's reading levels in relation to each other; located in *Assessment Forms*

Code (a reading record) Using a copy of the benchmark text, you record a student's oral reading errors, self-corrections, and other behaviors

Coding and Scoring Errors at-a-Glance A chart containing a brief summary of how to code and score oral reading errors (see inside back cover and *Assessment Forms*)

Comprehension (as in reading) The process of constructing meaning while reading a text

Comprehension conversation Part Two of the Benchmark Assessment in which the student shares his understanding of the text

Core reading program (see basal reading program)

► **D**

Diagnostic assessment A reading assessment designed to identify strengths and weaknesses in knowledge of specific language elements

► **E**

Error A reader's response that is not consistent with the text and that is *not* self-corrected

► **F**

F & P Calculator/Stopwatch A device that will calculate the reading time, reading rate, accuracy rate, and self-correction ratio for a reading

Fiction A story created from the imagination

Fluency (as in reading) The way an oral reading sounds, including phrasing, intonation, pausing, stress, rate, and integration of the first five factors

Font The style and size of type (alphabet characters) in a printed piece

► **G**

Genre A category of texts that share a particular form, common attributes, or content

Gradient of reading difficulty (see text gradient)

Guide for Observing and Noting Reading Behaviors Lists questions a teacher should ask himself or herself about the ways a student is processing or problem solving texts; located in *Assessment Forms*

► **H**

Hard reading level The level at which the student reads the text aloud with less than 90% accuracy (levels A–K) or less than 95% accuracy (levels L–Z)

Holistic scoring A score that reflects overall performance rather than counting items

► **I**

Independent reading level The level at which the student reads the text with 95% or higher accuracy and excellent or satisfactory comprehension (levels A–K) or 98% or higher accuracy with excellent or satisfactory comprehension (levels L–Z)

Individual instruction The teacher working with one student

Insertion (as in error in reading) A word added during oral reading that is not in the text

Instructional reading level At levels A–K, the level at which the student reads the text with 90–94% accuracy and excellent or satisfactory comprehension; or 95% or higher accuracy and limited comprehension. At levels L–Z, the level at which the student reads the text with 95–97% accuracy and excellent or satisfactory comprehension; or 98% or higher accuracy and limited comprehension.

Interactive read-aloud The teacher reading aloud to a group of students and inviting them to think and talk about the text before, during, and after reading

Intervention Intensive additional instruction for students not progressing as rapidly as expected; usually one-on-one tutoring or small-group (one-on-three) teaching

► **K**

Key understandings (in benchmark books) Important ideas within (literal), beyond (implied), or about (determined through critical analysis) the text that are necessary to comprehension

► **L**

Leveled books Texts designated along a gradient from level A (easiest) to level Z (hardest)

Literature discussion Students talking to each other about a text, either in a small group or with the whole class

Longitudinal Record of Reading Progress A graph showing a student's progress through reading levels across multiple grades; located in *Assessment Forms* book and CD-ROM and on Student Folders

▶ **M**

M (meaning) One of three sources of information that readers use (MSV: meaning, language structure, visual information). Meaning, the semantic system of language, refers to meaning derived from words, meaning across a text or texts, and meaning from personal experience or knowledge.

Minilesson A brief, focused lesson on any aspect of reading or writing, usually involving the whole class or a small group

▶ **N**

Nonfiction A text whose primary purpose is to convey information and facts that are accurate

▶ **O**

Omission (as in error) A word left out or skipped during oral reading

Optional assessments A selection of Phonics and Word Analysis plus Vocabulary Assessments designed to target specific areas of literacy knowledge; located in *Assessment Forms* book and CD-ROM

Oral reading (in Benchmark Assessment) Part II of the Benchmark Assessment during which the student reads a text aloud while the teacher codes the reading

▶ **P**

Phonics The study and teaching of letters and their related sounds as they function within words

Phonics and Word Analysis Assessments A set of optional assessments that evaluates letter knowledge, early literacy concepts, high frequency words, phonological awareness, letter-sound relationships, and word structure; located in *Assessment Forms* book and CD-ROM

Preprimer A beginning text used to teach reading; usually the first books read in a basal reading program

Primer An early reading text; follows preprimers and precedes the grade 1 text in a basal reading program

Processing (as in reading) The mental operations involved in constructing meaning from written language

Prompt (in Benchmark Assessment) A question, direction, or statement designed to encourage the student to say more about a topic during a comprehension conversation

▶ **Q**

Quarterly Assessment Summary A form that compiles Assessment Summary results from assessment conferences conducted four times during a school year; located in *Assessment Forms* book and CD-ROM

▶ **R**

Reading graph A graph that charts a student or students' progress through leveled books (see the Annual Record of Reading Progress and the Longitudinal Record of Reading Progress)

Reading interview An optional assessment containing questions to gain information about a student's reading preferences and reading history; located in *Assessment Forms* book and CD-ROM

Reading Rate (WPM) The number of words a student reads per minute, either orally (as in Benchmark Assessment) or silently

Reading record (in Benchmark Assessment) The transcript of the text on which oral reading is coded

Recording Form The form on which oral reading, the comprehension conversation, and the writing about reading assessment for a text are coded and scored. There is a Recording Form for each book in the Benchmark Assessment System. All are located in *Assessment Forms* book and CD-ROM.

Recommended Placement level The level the teacher, after taking into consideration all data gathered through Benchmark Assessment, decides is appropriate for reading instruction

Repetition (in oral reading) The reader saying a word, phrase, or section of the text more than once

Rubric A scoring tool that relies on descriptions of response categories for evaluation

Running words (in Benchmark Assessment) The number of words read aloud and coded during Part One Oral Reading

▶ **S**

S (structure) One of three sources of information that readers use (MSV: meaning, language structure, visual information). Language structure refers to the way words are put together in phrases and sentences (syntax or grammar).

Scoring and Analysis at-a-Glance A brief summary of the steps in scoring the three parts of a Benchmark Assessment: oral reading, comprehension conversation, and writing about reading; located in *Assessment Forms* book and CD-ROM

Scoring a reading record (in Benchmark Assessment) Counting coded errors and self corrections, which allows you to calculate *accuracy rate* and *self-correction ratio* on the Recording Form. The Form also provides space for a general *fluency score* (levels C–N) and *reading rate* (levels J–N).

Searching The reader looking for information in order to read accurately, self-correct, or understand a text

Self-correction ratio The proportion of errors the reader corrects himself

Shared and performance reading The teacher and students reading together (or in parts) a text that they know well

Silent reading The reader reading the text to herself

Six Dimensions Fluency Rubric A rubric for evaluating oral reading fluency on six dimensions: pausing, phrasing, stress, intonation, rate, and the combination of these, integration; located in *Assessment Forms* book and CD-ROM

Small-group reading instruction The teacher working with students brought together because they are similar enough in reading development to teach in a small group; guided reading

Sounding out (in Benchmark Reading Assessment) Pronouncing the sounds of the letters in a word as a step in reading the word

Spelling aloud (in Benchmark Reading Assessment) Naming the letters in a word rather than reading the word

Standardized Remaining essentially the same across multiple instances

Substitution (as in error in reading) The reader reading aloud one (incorrect) word for another

▶ **T**

Text gradient A twenty-six-point (A–Z) text-rating scale of difficulty in which each text level, from the easiest at level A to the most challenging at level Z, represents a small but significant increase in difficulty over the previous level. The gradient correlates these levels to grade levels.

Told (in Benchmark Reading Assessment) The teacher telling the reader a word he cannot read

Tri-annual Assessment Summary A form that compiles Assessment Summary results from assessment conferences conducted three times during a school year; located in *Assessment Forms* book and CD-ROM

▶ **V**

V (visual information) One of three sources of information that readers use (MSV: meaning, language structure, visual information). Visual information refers to the letters that represent the sounds of language and way they are combined (spelling patterns) to create words; visual information at the sentence level includes punctuation.

Vocabulary Words and their meanings

Vocabulary Assessments A set of optional assessments that evaluates a student's word knowledge (concept words, vocabulary in context), understanding of word relationships (synonyms, antonyms, roots, analogies), and ability to derive the precise meaning of words in the context of a short book (vocabulary in context); located in *Assessment Forms* book and CD-ROM

▶ **W**

Where-to-Start Word Test A graded list of increasingly difficult words. The number of words the student reads aloud accurately is converted into an approximate level for beginning Benchmark Assessment. Located in *Assessment Forms* book and CD-ROM.

Whole-group instruction The teacher teaching a lesson to an entire class or a large part of it

Writing Students engaging in the writing process and producing pieces of their own writing in many genres

Writing about reading Students responding to reading a text by writing and sometimes drawing

▶ **Y**

You Try It (in Benchmark Reading Assessment) A teacher prompt that directs a student to make an attempt at reading a word during oral reading